FAMILY-SCHOOL COLLABORATION MANUAL

Howard M. Weiss, PhD

Fran Schwartz, PhD, LCSW

Martha Edwards, PhD

a project of

THE CENTER FOR THE DEVELOPING CHILD AND FAMILY

Acknowledgements

This Manual is the product of a collaborative effort. Several people have contributed their energy and creativity to its development. Ifaat Qureshi tirelessly formatted and edited the earliest drafts. Egda Del Valle Delaney, MSW and Mindy Zelen, PhD each drafted sessions for early versions of the Manual. Ariela Rutkin-Becker enthusiastically and expertly re-edited and reformatted the entire manuscript and offered many valuable ideas for improving the content and layout. Leah Bernhardi thoroughly and painstakingly reviewed the manuscript, asked wise questions and reformatted the final draft. Zina Rutkin, PhD brought her fine and astute eye to the editing and revision of the final version.

We thank the teachers, administrators, children and families who welcomed us into their schools and worked with us in honing the core ideas for the Manual.

Dear Educators,

Welcome to the CKCC Family-School Collaboration Manual. This manual provides a comprehensive sequence of sessions to help schools, families, and students develop more educationally-meaningful conversations that in turn can ultimately lead to improved academic performance for students.

Contained within is a framework for conceptualizing home-school relationships as interlocking systems and the implications for how schools and families can work together. The sessions provide concrete strategies and activities that school staff, parents, and students use to create positive family-school relationships and, ultimately, better educational experiences for children.

Understanding the daily reality of life in schools, including the limited amount of time allotted to professional development in many settings, we encourage you to tailor your use of this manual to your school's needs. While adhering to the scope and sequence delineated is one way to use this manual, it is also possible to identify one or more specific series of sessions that address current issues in your school, and to implement those without having engaged in the preceding sessions. To that end, the Table of Contents which follows outlines specific questions for each session. Feel free to use the Table of Contents to guide your school's use of the manual.

We hope you find this manual helpful and user-friendly as you embark on the process of strengthening a collaborative approach in your school!

Sincerely,

The CKCC Team

TABLE OF CONTENTS

SECTION 1: <u>OVERVIEW: THE BASICS</u> 1

I. Introduction 2

II. The Cornerstones: Systems and Collaboration 6

    SESSION 1: *What is meant by collaboration?* 6

    SESSION 2: *What are systems and why are they important to family-School collaboration?* 17

III. The Context: School Climate 24

    SESSION 3: *How can we see school climate as a frame for family-school collaboration?* 24

    SESSION 4: *What kinds of activities foster a collaborative climate?* 32

SECTION 2: <u>NEEDS ASSESSMENT: GETTING STARTED</u> 45

    SESSION 5: *What are the benefits of a needs assessment, and how is data collected?* 46

    SESSION 6: *How do we use the results of the needs assessments to shape our decision-making processes?* 56

SECTION 3: <u>THE COLLABORATIVE APPROACH: THE MEETING FLOW STEPS</u> 73

I. The Collaborative Process 74

    SESSION 7: *How can we prepare for the realities of family-school collaboration?* 74

II. Finding Facts 85

    SESSION 8: *What is fact-finding, and how can interviewing skills help?* 85

III. Blocking Blame 98

    SESSION 9: *How do blaming statements undermine collaboration?* 98

    SESSION 10: *What techniques can help to block blame?* 104

IV. Creating a Plan 115

    SESSION 11: *How are plans created at the end of a collaborative problem-solving meeting?* 115

SECTION 4: THE CORE ACTIVITIES: CLIMATE-BUILDING ... 129

I. Orientation ... 130

SESSION 12: *Why is a family-school orientation important?* ... 130

SESSION 13: *What does a specific family-school orientation look like?* ... 145

SESSION 14: *What are the final steps of family-school orientation planning?* ... 150

II. Family-Teacher Conferences ... 160

SESSION 15: *How do we transform parent-teacher conferences into family-teacher conferences that include the child?* ... 160

III. Family-School Problem-Solving Meetings ... 177

SESSION 16: *What is a family-school problem-solving meeting?* ... 177

SESSION 17: *How can we adapt the meeting flow steps to family-school problem-solving meetings?* ... 186

SESSION 18: *What are the final steps of a family-school problem-solving meeting?* ... 197

SESSION 19: *How do we implement a successful problem-solving meeting for multiple families?* ... 209

SECTION 5: ELECTIVE CLIMATE-BUILDING: NEW OPPORTUNITIES FOR COLLABORATION ... 215

SESSION 20: *How do we review issues in our school from a collaborative point of view?* ... 216

SESSION 21: *How do we implement a successful elective climate-building activity?* ... 225

SESSION 22: *How can we collaborate with families at home?* ... 237

SESSION 23: *How can we develop elective collaborative activities with high school populations?* ... 258

SESSION 24: *How can we reach populations with special needs?* ... 270

SESSION 25: *How do we embed family-school collaboration into our school's calendar?* ... 278

SECTION 6: SUSTAINING THE MOMENTUM: DEEPENING INVESTMENT ... 289

I. Making It Stick: Institutionalizing Collaboration ... 290

SESSION 26: *How can we institutionalize a collaborative approach?* ... 290

II. Action Research: Reflective Conversations about Collaboration ... 301

SESSION 27: *What is an action research approach to feedback of evaluation research?* ... 301

SECTION 1

OVERVIEW: THE BASICS

I. Introduction

What is CKCC?

Competent Kids, Caring Communities, or CKCC for short, reflects a systemic approach to education. "Competent Kids" learn both academic and social-emotional skills, which reinforce one another. "Caring Communities," consisting of the whole school, its families, and even the neighborhood, provide an environment that supports this learning.

CKCC focuses on helping schools develop a **collaborative climate** that fosters relationships among school staff, parents, and children in order to maximize children's social-emotional and academic growth. By working in tandem with school staff, and utilizing available structures and resources within schools, CKCC works to find ways to connect every family directly to their children's learning experience. Thus, the term "collaboration" describes both *how* we work as well as *what* we promote.

CKCC consists of two components: (1) a Family-School Collaboration component, coming out of the work originated in 1981 by Howard M. Weiss, Ph.D. and Arthur Maslow, M.S.W.;[1] and (2) a Social-Emotional component, developed in 1990 by Marcia Stern, Psy.D. These two components are meant to be implemented together as they mutually reinforce one another and support children's academic success.

The Family-School Collaboration Component

The goal of the Family-School component of CKCC is the development of collaborative family-school relationships characterized by mutual trust, regular communication, and cooperation. Over 20 years, we trained thousands of teachers, administrators, guidance counselors, psychologists and social workers to collaborate with families. We don't ask school staff to do extra work in order to create these collaboration relationships. Rather, we help them learn to do what they would already be doing differently, using new models for meeting with parents and students and for creating school-wide activities. As school staff come to understand the power of family-school collaboration, they begin to consistently ask themselves and others how the family can be used as a resource for solving problems, celebrating success, and supporting learning.

When our work was first conceived, parents were typically not viewed as partners in their child's education. School staff often perceived parents as uncaring and uninvolved. Families, in turn, saw school staff as remote and unavailable to hear their concerns. In the recent past, schools have witnessed a new wave of parent involvement initiatives in a range of

---

[1] This work was done as the Family-School Collaboration Project at the Ackerman Institute for the Family which became the Center for Family-School Collaboration in 1995.

areas from school governance and restructuring to decision-making about curriculum and instruction. True collaboration, however, results in shared goals and a mutually enhancing family-school relationship where each child's family is meaningfully involved in his or her education.

Our work initially focused on the problems of individual children, which were addressed through conducting family-school problem-solving meetings. Gradually, we began to take a more preventative approach. We helped schools build collaborative *climates,* which both reduced the number of challenging behaviors and lay positive foundations for dealing with difficulties when they did arise.

Collaborative work can help families and schools set and achieve goals to improve the school environment. When the environment sends a message that family-school collaboration is valued, new opportunities for family-school collaboration emerge. As school staff, families and children discuss school issues like inappropriate behavior, share concerns about educational and social problems, and engage in joint educational activities, all are empowered to define the mission and values of their school.

Whether the focus is on preventing problems or helping to resolve them, our aim has always been to help schools work as a team with families and children to create supportive, warm and enhancing relations that maximize the cognitive, academic, social, and emotional growth of children.

Objectives of CKCC Family-School Collaboration

1. To assess the needs of the school[2] regarding family-school relationships;
2. To help school staff understand school life from a systems perspective;
3. To help schools productively utilize school staff, families and children as resources in new ways;
4. To help schools transform existing school activities (family-school meetings, family-teacher conferences, orientation meetings) into events which are specifically designed to build an interactive, collaborative climate;
5. To help schools design (elective) collaborative climate building activities to address their specific needs or concerns;
6. To help schools employ a collaborative approach to school-wide and classroom events by involving parents, staff, and children in each stage from planning to implementation to evaluation;
7. To use evaluation as a part of the ongoing collaborative change process with school personnel as active participants.

---

[2] Throughout this manual, when the word "school" is used, it is understood to potentially apply to entire networks or districts as well as individual schools.

What can I expect from this manual?

The manual is comprised of a series of sessions that build on each other. We begin with an overview of key concepts such as systems, collaboration, and school climate. We then introduce a process for assessing the current state of collaboration in your school and identifying areas for which CKCC's approach might be helpful. Next, we explore the "Meeting Flow Steps:" the essential elements of CKCC's collaborative process. We then use these steps as tools to transform traditional school events such as orientations and parent-teacher conferences into collaborative activities. Having experienced collaborative planning and implementation of school activities, you will be ready to create elective climate-building activities that address your unique setting. Finally, we will contemplate ways to sustain the collaborative momentum you've been working hard to build!

Who should use this manual?

This manual should be used by: (a) national-, state-, district-, and school-based *educators* (i.e., superintendents, principals, administrators, teachers, and support service staff), (b) *mental health workers* (psychologists, social workers, guidance counselors, and evaluators), (c) organizational and educational *consultants*, and (d) educational *planners*.

How do I use this manual?

CKCC recommends that each setting appoint a Facilitator to lead school staff through the exercises in this manual. While the activities were developed to be delivered sequentially, and tend to yield the most powerful results when they are, CKCC recognizes that, due to the time constraints faced by many schools, this may not be feasible. Consequently, it is also possible to tailor the order, number, and types of activities, depending upon the needs of the particular school.

CKCC provides training to Facilitators to support them in this process.

Sessions with staff can be scheduled either before-school, after-school, on a weekend, or as part of a professional development series. It is suggested that each participant have her own small binder to store the useful wealth of information that will be distributed in the form of handouts throughout the course of the sessions.

The following graphic cues are intended to help guide the Facilitator in preparation and delivery of the sessions:

Think About It. This cue signifies that reflection questions will follow. Typically, respondents will share their answers to these questions out loud, and they might in turn be recorded by the Facilitator.

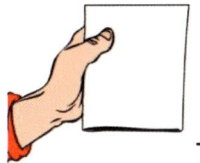

This cue invites the Facilitator to record participant responses on the writing board available. The cue will be followed by a description of what the chart should look like, if applicable.

This cue signifies a distribution of handout(s).

This cue is followed by text to be paraphrased out loud. Please feel free to put the subsequent text, **found in this font,** in your own words. Because of the prevalence of speaking cues throughout the manual, this graphic will typically be found only once per an individual activity. The **font**, however, will be found wherever there is material to summarize out loud to the group.

This is a tip that is meant to help you in the preparation of your words or in the distribution of materials.

Text found inside this sort of box is typically supplemental material to guide discussion, such as possible responses for a group's *Think About It* or a "problem and solution" guide for a specific activity.

II. The Cornerstones: Systems and Collaboration

SESSION 1: What is meant by collaboration?

Rationale:

This session introduces the concept of collaboration as it is used by the CKCC team. Our approach differs from traditional parent involvement efforts, i.e. parenting education, parent volunteerism, and parents as audience in two key ways. First, rather than just inviting parents into the school to teach them specific skills or recruit them for specific tasks, we help school staffs develop a meaningful dialogue with all parents-whether they can come to the school or not- about their child's educational experience. Second, we help schools create a three-way partnership among themselves, their students and their students' families that affects the climate of the school as a whole. Students are routinely included as active participants in all meetings and events that pertain to them.

Collaborative partnerships have three key elements:

- Shared and mutually developed goals.
- Each person including the student has a clear, agreed upon part in enriching the student's learning experience at school and at home.
- All parties work together acknowledging the distinct contribution and expertise of all involved individuals.

Goals

- To define collaboration as it is used by the CKCC team.

- To explore examples of collaborative vs. traditional modes of solving problems and conducting school meetings.

Handouts/Materials

- *Family-School Songs*
- *Three Levels of Positive Family-School Relationships*
- *Examples of Positive Family-School Relationships*
- *Levels of Positive Family-School Relationships: Self-Evaluation Form*
- White board/Smart Board or chart paper

Introduction

We are about to embark on our first session in a series of workshops in family-school collaboration. Everyone from administrators to politicians to students themselves talks about the critical impact of parental involvement in schools. They note the improved attendance, attitudes and academic performance of students whose parents take an active interest in their education and are engaged in a meaningful dialogue with their schools. But it is easier to describe the outcomes of such family-school partnerships than to actually create them. Over the next several sessions, we will be learning a step-by-step process for creating a truly collaborative climate in your school.

Warm-Up

1. Distribute *Family-School Songs* Handout #1. Ask participants to look through the list and identify the one (or suggest another) which best exemplifies their school's relationships with families.

   Warm-up Songs:
   - Ain't it a shame
   - Sorry
   - Take this job and shove it
   - Getting to know you
   - Mutual admiration society
   - Can't get no satisfaction

2. Go around the circle asking each participant to share his/her response and to say a word or two about why he/she chose that particular song.

3. Note whether most participants chose songs that positively or negatively describe family/school relationships and summarize key reasons for choices.

Activity I. Reflection

INSTRUCTIONS

1. Say: **Think for a moment privately about a positive relationship with a family that you have had which best illustrates how you think families and schools should work together. Then, in your own mind, identify the core elements of this successful relationship.**

For example, in my experience...(tell about a good working relationship that you have had with a family. Core elements in that experience might be mutual trust and respect.)

2. Reporting out: **Now, let's share some of the core elements of a good relationship with a student's family which you identified.**

3. 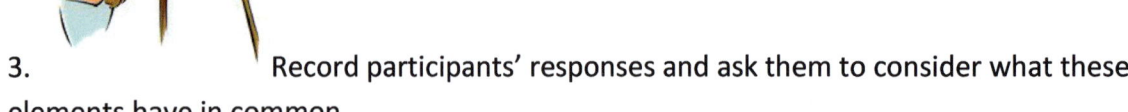 Record participants' responses and ask them to consider what these elements have in common.

4. Say: **What do you think these elements have in common?**

Answers might include:

- Parent-teacher united front
- Same message to student
- They felt respected professionally
- Their advice was taken
- There was openness
- It was non-attacking, non-blaming and non-defensive.

Activity II. Levels of Collaboration

INSTRUCTIONS

1. Say: **We are going to explore different types of positive family-school relationships so you can get a clearer idea of how a collaborative relationship differs from the others.**

2. Distribute *Three Levels of Positive Family-School Relationships* Handout #2. Review the handout with participants. Ask them to identify differences in the roles of the teacher, parent and student in each level.

3. Say: **It is important to further explain and define positive family-school relationships by examples.**

4. Distribute *Examples of Positive Family-School Relationships* Handout #3 and read these examples with participants.

5. Ask participants to provide their own examples of collaborative, cooperative or coordinated.

6. *Think About It.* Break participants into small groups and ask them to focus on the following questions:

- *What strikes you most about the difference between the traditional and collaborative ways of doing a specific event?*

- *What might be the hardest aspect of making the transition from traditional to collaborative in your schools?*

7. Have the groups report out. Record their statements and identify common themes and shared issues among the groups. Inform the participants that they're going to have more opportunities to deal with these issues later.

8. Say: **Now that you've gotten a sense of different levels of interaction between families and school, let's go back and assess where you think your school is at this point.**

Activity III. Self-Evaluation

INSTRUCTIONS

1. Distribute *Levels of Positive Family-School Relationships: Self Evaluation Form* Handout #4.

2. Ask participants to complete this form indicating where they think their schools are now-- NOT them as individual school staff, and not where they would like to see themselves.

3. Ask participants: What are the obstacles that block increased collaboration?

SESSION 1
Handout 1

Family-School Songs

Ain't It a Shame

Sorry

Take This Job and Shove It

Getting to Know You

Mutual Admiration Society

Can't Get No Satisfaction

SESSION 1
Handout 2

Three Levels of Positive Family-School Relationships

The Coordinated

1. Families and schools act independently of each other.

2. There is a lack of regular communication between the systems.

3. Parents may attend special events.

The Cooperative

1. Families and schools generally have a one-way flow of communication going from school to parents.

2. Parents support teacher's role as expert and do what teacher recommends.

3. Parents may assist the teacher on special projects.

The Collaborative

1. Families and schools generally have three-way interactions among parents, teachers and children.

2. There is an ongoing discussion about the child's needs and a sense of working together for common concerns.

3. Parents and teachers not only work together routinely but also identify and share specific goals. Their connections and interactions are characterized by give and take from both sides.

SESSION 1
Handout 3

Examples of Positive Family-School Relationships

The Coordinated

1. Parents come to school as audience members for events like school plays.

2. Teachers do not know about areas of a family's or child's potential interest and/or about how a family may have applied learning that the child acquired in the classroom. Often this information is shared when discussing a problem that has arisen.

3. Parents attend regularly scheduled conferences but otherwise obtain information about their child's school life through the child, from reviewing the child's schoolwork and from notes sent home by the school.

The Cooperative

1. Parents come to school to help out in classroom. They may volunteer to help the teacher with special events by chaperoning school trips and making costumes for a school play.

2. Teacher asks parents to do certain activities with children at home (read to them, help with homework) and parents comply.

3. Parents seek the teacher's advice about how to improve their child's school performance.

The Collaborative

1. Parents, teachers and children plan and implement family-school activities together based on each of their strengths, available time and interest. Activities can vary (i.e., multicultural programs, family-reading).

2. Parents, teachers and children all know each other's goals for the school year.

3. Parents and teachers work together to decide what role each should take in helping children. For example, it may be mutually decided that parents can help by making calls to other parents at night because she or he is not available during the day due to work commitments).

4. Teachers seek parents' input about what would be effective ways to help their child at school.

SESSION 1
Handout 4

Levels of Positive Family-School Relationships: Self-Evaluation Form

Please read through the following possible positive family-school interactions and place a check next to those that describe the current practices in your school. Be sure to complete this form from the point of view of the school overall NOT for you as an individual school staff member or as how you would like to see the school in the future.

The Coordinated

___ Parents come to school for events like school plays.

___ Teachers and parents do not communicate regularly but each fulfills their roles with the children responsibly.

___ Parents attend orientation meetings which inform them about expectations, rules and homework procedures and answer their questions.

___ Parents attend open-school night.

___ Parents learn primarily about their children's school experiences and progress from report cards and parent teacher conferences.

___ Teachers contact parents about individual children only when there is a problem.

The Cooperative

___ Parents are routinely asked to sign homework.

___ Parents know teachers' goals for their children.

___ At the teacher's request, parents help children with certain activities at home.

___ Teachers inform parents about classroom activities through regular newsletters.

___ Teachers are readily available to meet with parents who have concerns.

___ Parents play a range of roles as helpers and organizers of events within the school.

The Collaborative

___ Children are routinely invited to attend parent-teacher meetings.

___ Parents are asked early in the school year for information about their children.

___ Parents and teachers share their goals for children's education and recognize ones they have in common.

___ Parents, teachers and children all contribute to plans for the child's educational progress.

___ Parents feel welcome to initiate ideas, materials or topics for classroom learning activities.

___ Teachers solicit parents' advice about how to improve a child's learning or behavior.

End of Session 1

SESSION 2: What are systems and why are they important in relation to family-school collaboration?

Rationale:

CKCC utilizes a systemic approach in its work with families and schools. This approach views the family and the school as systems of interacting and interdependent parts. For the school, these parts include teachers, support staff, aides, clerical workers, administrators, students, their families and the broader community. For the family, the system includes at least the parents/guardians and children, but may also include grandparents, aunts, uncles, and others. As systems, families and schools have readily discernible patterns of communication governed by often-unstated rules (or norms), assumptions, and needs.

A change in one person's behavior does not occur in isolation. Rather, it affects the behavior of others in the system as well. For instance, if a teacher alters the way she interacts with students, this may change not only her relationship to the students but also indirectly her relationship or the child's relationship with his/her parents as the shifts reverberate through students to their families.

As a pupil at a school and a child in a family, a student is a member of two systems, the family system and the system of the school. Each of these can operate very differently and pull the child in different directions. *Our work aims to create a third collaborative system out of these two distinct and sometimes disparate systems.*

Only then can students feel supported by the cooperation of the adults in their lives and can the family and school work with each other to provide maximum resources for the student. The more families and schools work together, the better it is for the student.

Why is an understanding of systems so important?

What makes the concept of systems so critical to our work is that a system itself is more powerful than its individual members. A system is more than the composite characteristics of a group of individuals. People who, when separated might act differently take on certain repeated, recognizable patterns of behavior when they are together: they become a system. Failure to acknowledge and to work with respect for the power of the school or the family system can undermine even the most well intended change efforts.

Goals
- To understand the basic concept of systems.
- To apply systemic thinking to participants' own school experiences.
- To appreciate the role of every member of a system in improving students' school experiences.

Handouts/Materials
- *What is a System?*
- White board/Smart Board or chart paper

Introduction

One of the keys to facilitating family-school collaboration is understanding how the family and the school function independently and together as systems. In this session we are going to explore a basic concept of family-school collaboration: the concept of systems. As a way of beginning to think about systemic relationships between families and schools, I'd like you to take a minute to reflect about your family's relationship to the school when you were growing up.

Activity I. Reflection

INSTRUCTIONS

1. **Say: Do you think your own family and the school you attended when you were young worked well together or not?**

   Let's have a show of hands: How many of you think they worked well together? Ok. How many think they did not work well together? How do you explain the success or difficulties in these family-school relationships?

2. Comment on the relative numbers of those who think they worked well and those who think they did not.

3. Explain to participants that we will return to these observations later in the session and ask them to remember what they thought.

Activity II. Lecturette

INSTRUCTIONS

1. 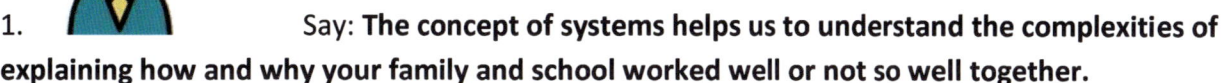 Say: **The concept of systems helps us to understand the complexities of explaining how and why your family and school worked well or not so well together.**

2. 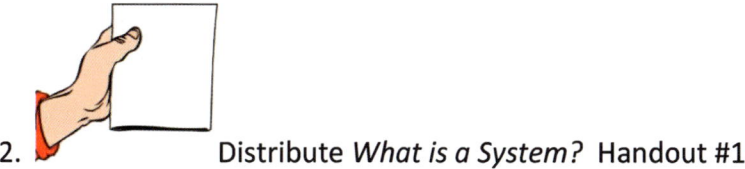 Distribute *What is a System?* Handout #1.

3. Say: **A system can be simply defined as: two or more parts and the relationship between them. In the nuclear family, parents and children are the elements of the family system, which is also defined by the nature of the relationship between these elements or members. The system of the school includes teachers, administrators, guidance counselors, psychologists, social workers, aides, custodians, security guards, cafeteria workers, volunteers and others. We can also conceive of the family and the school forming a larger and more complex system.**

   Using a systemic approach involves considering situations with a particular point of view:

   - **It involves giving emphasis to organization, i.e., the relationship structure between or among parts. A system (like a family or a school) is composed of a set of interdependent parts.**
     a. A change in one part of the system effects change in other parts (e.g., When teachers decide to give more homework to improve academic achievement, this change may influence how a student and his family interact around bedtime routines.)
     b. When we emphasize the relationships, we give attention to *hierarchy, alliances, coalitions,* and *triangles* that define the connections among the members of a system.

   - **We also concentrate on patterned rather than linear relationships.**
     a. Causality is seen as complex and circular, rather than linear.
     b. We seek to identify patterns or interactional sequences that repeat over time.

19

- **We consider events in a context. Behavior is understood as occurring in relationship contexts.**
    - a. For example, children may receive different cues about how to respond to aggression at home and at school and their behavior may be deemed as appropriate in one context and inappropriate in the other.

- **Systems regulate and control the behavior of the component parts.**
    - a. Overt or covert rules or norms govern patterns of interaction including communication and feedback. For example, it is not uncommon for the normative interaction pattern or style of a child's family system to clash with a classroom system style. One might be quite open while another might be quite closed.
    - b. There is a balance of tension between stability and change with new information creating the potential for change.
    - c. The structures of systems vary in their degrees of flexibility (e.g., of roles, problem-solving practices and styles of interaction). For example, the *boundary* of a system, which defines what is inside or outside the system, can vary in its degree of *permeability* or rigidity.

- **We focus on interactional patterns and sequences within and between family and school systems to see how a problem is maintained in a particular system. For example, we might ask how the family and school systems influence each other to maintain the child's problem.**
    - a. We take the position that no one is to blame for a child's difficulties. Rather, everyone contributes in some way and changes can occur in varying ways in one or both systems. All have contributions to make toward the solution of problems.

Activity III. Case Example

INSTRUCTIONS

1. Say: **Let's take the following case example and consider the implications for the child by applying systems concepts. Use the diagram of the family-school systems to think through the issues.** (Read the following case example out loud, have it written or projected onto a screen at the front of the room, or have slips of it printed out on participants' tables beforehand).

Case Example: Johnny Norton

The Norton family is quite secretive about its own business. Johnny, a 4th grader, attends a school that emphasizes sharing and openness between adults and children. Johnny's teacher has called the parents about her concern that Johnny does not participate in "circle time" where the children typically talk about their home experiences.

2. *Think About It.* Ask the participants to reflect on the following:

- *Explain from a system's perspective why Johnny might not be sharing.*

- *Explain what differences between patterns of interaction at home and school might mean to John as a member of both systems.*

- *How might you intervene to effect change?*

SESSION 2
Handout 1

What is a System?
The Family is a System.
The School is a System.

A system is composed of two or more parts and the relationship between them. When we look at a family and at a complex organization like a school as systems we give special emphasis to the *relationship* between its parts. The people in these systems and the positions they occupy are the components of the system that are connected by their *patterns of relationship,* observable as patterns of interaction. Each system has shared rules or norms about how people should interact, as well as shared values of meanings. Each system has a *boundary* which distinguishes who is and is not a part of the system and which may vary in the *degree of permeability* and *rigidity* it allows for passage of people or information across it. Boundary permeability between and among members, subsystems and the total system determines the rigidity or flexibility of interactions within a system and between one system and another.

- People in systems are interconnected and interdependent.
- A system is more than the composite characteristics of a group of individuals.
- People who when separated might act differently take on certain repeated and recognizable patterns of behavior when they are together --they become a system.
- Change in one part of the system can create change in other parts. Causality is seen as multi-determined and circular rather than linear A causes B.
- The family and the school are each distinctive systems with their own rules, patterns of interactions, assumptions, and needs. Systems vary in their degree of flexibility of roles, problem-solving practices, and styles.
- When we consider events involving the children, parents and/or school, we must always recognize the importance of the context. We consider behaviors in their relationship contexts.
- A system regulates and controls the behavior of its members or component parts through its norms. Control of the system is maintained by its structures, including patterns of communication and feedback. The system is always in a dynamic balance between stability and change (like a tight rope walker moving constantly in order to maintain his balance). New information creates the potential for change.
The child belongs to both systems. They can work well together for the child or they can work against each other and undermine the child's educational and emotional growth.

End of Session 2

III. The Context: School Climate

SESSION 3: How can we see school climate as a frame for family-school collaboration?

Rationale:

In collaborative work, it is essential to proactively establish relationships between all families and the school. These connections both prevent future problems and lay a positive foundation for dealing with problems when they do arise.

At the core of this work is the concept of school *climate*, which becomes the context for teachers', students', and families' views of and interactions with each other. *Climate building* is a term that can be used to generally describe a long and steady process of shaping the physical and social-emotional properties of the school environment. The purpose of this process is to send clear and consistent messages that the family and school are working together for the good of the child. Climate-building activities can unleash previously unavailable resources in families, students and school staffs as they become less defensive, more trusting, and more open to collaboration. It is important to highlight that *small changes towards collaboration can have a very powerful positive impact* on routine interaction patterns and on the thoughts and feelings of educators, students and parents about one another.

As school staff come to understand that the climate is not a given, but rather can be changed to correspond with the values and messages it wants to convey to parents and children, staff become increasingly interested in examining and, when appropriate, reshaping the school's current climate.

Through a series of core interventions, called *climate-building activities*, schools are able to generate warm, inviting and respectful climates which are conducive to family-school collaboration. These interventions do not require the school to add new activities to their calendar of events. Instead they offer schools new ways of organizing already existing activities. When school staff has learned to implement collaborative climate-building activities, it can then use similar processes to address a wide range of issues.

There are two types of interventions: the core and the elective. Core interventions include orientations, family-teacher conferences, and family-school problem solving meetings for groups or individual families and children. Elective interventions are specifically designed to address the needs and issues of individual schools. They can range from multi-family problem solving meetings to prevent retention to school-wide workshops to help families and students prepare for standardized tests.

It is important to emphasize that climate-building activities are a means for dealing with important educational issues and concerns, and are not events implemented for the sake of parental involvement alone.

Goals
- To articulate basic concepts of school climate.
- To assess and think about ways to change participants' own school climate.

Handouts/Materials
- *Components of Climate*
- *Assessment of School Climate*
- White board/Smart Board or chart paper

Introduction

Say: **Before we can begin to actively alter relationships between the family and school, we need to think about what the school environment is like for children, families and teachers. We will identify key aspects of this environment and discuss how they can be shaped to promote collaboration.**

First, we will start out with a warm-up activity. Then we will discuss the elements of school climate.

Warm-Up

1. Describe the climate for family-school relations in your school as though it were a weather condition. For example: "tropical with summer breezes," "very arid with few green patches," or "frigid with lots of ice and little sun."

2. Ask participants to share their reports on their schools. Briefly summarize the ways in which they view their schools.

3. Say: **We've talked about schools as having climates of their own, distinctive temperature and weather conditions. Organizations like schools do have climates or certain environmental tones of conditions. We need to know what they are before we can think about how to improve or change them.**

Activity I. Reflection

INSTRUCTIONS

1.  Say: **Think for a moment about a real school. Choose from these 3 options: the school you work in now, a school your child has attended or the school you attended as a child. Imagine yourself entering this building with a new pair of eyes and ears as a parent. What are the visual, verbal, non-verbal messages to you about the school's attitude to you/your child?**

What do the physical environment, signs and bulletin boards suggest about the school's interest in families?

2.  Have the participants share responses and list these. Identify themes and aspects of the environment that convey key messages.

3. *Think About It.* Using the list formulated above, point to each message and/or response. Ask participants to reflect on the following:

- *How, if at all, would you like to change one of the key messages listed to make the school feel more collaborative and welcoming to parents and children?*

- *What messages would you like the environment to convey?*

- *How do you think the school could do that?*

4. Say: **Before we can begin to change the messages, it's necessary to have a way of thinking about school environments and the messages they convey.**

Activity II. Components of Climate

INSTRUCTIONS

1. Say: **As we can see, the environment conveys very powerful messages to families and children about the school's willingness to collaborate with them and see them as partners. We can identify different aspects of the school environment or school climate, and begin to think about how these could be altered to make the environment more welcoming and comfortable for families and children.**

2. Distribute *"Components of Climate"* Handout #1. Ask participants to skim through the four components, highlighting:

- **Culture** - The message (values, norms, beliefs)
- **Milieu** - People and groups
- **Social System** - Patterns of interactions among people
- **Ecology** - Physical characteristics of the environment.

Activity III. Assessment of School Climate

INSTRUCTIONS

1. Say: **Now let's break into four small groups. Each group will represent a different constituency in your school e.g., students, parents, teachers and administrators.**

2. Distribute *Assessment of School Climate* Handout #2 to the participants in each group.

3. Say: **You will work together as a team using the conceptual framework we've discussed to identify key aspects of your school's climate. Specifically, for each of the 4 elements of school climate consider, and then record, how a parent, student, teacher or administrator (e.g., principal) might experience the climate of your school. Identify at least one aspect under each element about which you are proud and one aspect that suggests a need for improvement.**

4. Reporting Out: Say: **Now let's share observations about your school.**
Encourage participants to be concrete in their observations (i.e., they should note what they actually see that gives them information about the school's willingness to collaborate with parents and students to allow for shared decision making).

5. Say: **Now return to your groups and list changes in the climate that would make your school a more positive environment for you. Identify and list obstacles that might get in the way of making these changes on a piece of paper.**

SESSION 3
Handout 1

Components of Climate

CULTURE

Culture represents the values, norms and beliefs that are communicated. One message that can be relayed is that education is a shared family-school process. This message can be conveyed through particular curriculum units, like family trees, family stories, and cultural heritage. Another value that might be communicated is that the school and families both maintain *high standards* for effort and achievement in learning.

MILIEU

Milieu refers to the individuals and groups in the school. Groups can work together to create a collaborative atmosphere in the school. These groups can be comprised of the school staff, children and families. The groups can be comprised of the family-school team, and/or diverse ethnic/racial/cultural groups. A key question regarding the school climate is: How do we make our similarities and *differences* resources for the school?

SOCIAL SYSTEM

Social system describes the ways that people interact together. It is that part of the climate that includes patterns of communication like how participants communicate, and how they do what they do together. For example, how do teachers, students and parents share and build connections among themselves?

ECOLOGY

Ecology refers to the physical characteristics and objects of the school environment that convey messages to and about the people in this environment including what they value and how they interact with each other. This might include welcoming signs to school visitors, displays of children's academic and artistic work in the hallways, and family informational bulletin boards.

All of these elements contribute to the climate of the school. In essence, climate is a complex phenomenon integrating the message sent by everything that goes on in a school: The mission of the school, the characteristics of the members who make up the school, how the school feels to a visitor, a parent, a child or staff member, how the environment is organized, and the patterns of interaction among these various groups, which may range from whole school meetings to one-an-one teaching.

SESSION 3
Handout 2

Assessment of School Climate

Instructions: From the perspective of a student, parent, teacher or principal answer the questions for each element of climate. Try to identify at least one aspect within each category about which you are proud and one aspect that suggests a need for improvement.

Physical Environment (ECOLOGY): How would your constituency describe the physical appearance of the school (e.g., signs, bulletin boards, colors, seating)? What message does the physical environment convey to you about your value to and role in the school?

Individuals/Groups (MILIEU): Who are the people and groups in the school (e.g., ethno-racial identity, level of education, income level, etc.)? Who is acknowledged by the school? In what ways? Who is 'invisible' in the school?

Patterns of Interactions (SOCIAL SYSTEM): What are people doing? How are they interacting with each other and with you?

Values, norms, beliefs (CULTURE): What values, norms and beliefs are conveyed to you by the school, through your interactions with people in the school, and by the physical setting about:

- The school's missions and styles of operating?
- What the school expects of you?
- What the school expects children to achieve?

End of Session 3

SESSION 4: What kinds of activities foster a collaborative climate?

Rationale:

A collaborative school climate is a warm, welcoming and friendly atmosphere where individuals trust one another. Individuals feel valued, heard, and included in the educational process. Specific climate-building activities help to move collaboration forward.

Climate-building activities are comprised of core and elective activities. Four *core activities* serve to address the schools' efforts at creating a collaborative climate for staff, parents and children.

In addition, school staff work towards creating elective climate-building activities to address the specific needs, issues or concerns of the school. These activities can range in scale and magnitude. They can be in-class or school-wide activities.

Handouts/Materials

- *Basic Premises of Family-School Collaboration*
- *Core Activities*
- *Examples of Elective Activities*
- *Sample Academic Year Calendar*
- White board/Smart Board or chart paper

Goals

- To specify key elements of collaborative climate building.
- To identify basic core and elective climate-building activities.
- To appreciate how core activities can fit easily into the existing school calendar.

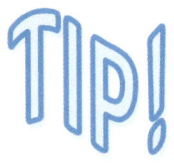

TIP!

> Check to see if the school/school(s) has its own blank academic year calendar. Otherwise, use the sample provided for you.

Activity I. Reflection

INSTRUCTIONS

1. *Think About It.* Ask participants to reflect privately about these two questions, being prepared to report out:

    • What would have to be present in a school for you to say unequivocally: "This is a collaborative climate!"?

    • What would you look for as signs that collaboration was occurring? These are signs that would make you feel comfortable in saying without hesitation that this is definitely a collaborative school.

2. Record participants' responses as they report out.

3. Ask participants to identify themes in the statements they've made. Highlight themes to emphasize three central characteristics of collaboration:

> 1. Developing shared goals and directions
> 2. Recognizing mutual responsibility and obligations for obtaining goals
> 3. Working together to achieve those goals with all participants contributing valuable and sometimes different skills and resources.

Activity II. Basic Premises for Collaborative Work

INSTRUCTIONS

1. Distribute *Basic Premises for Collaborative Work* Handout #1.

2. Say: **The broad themes we just identified rest on a concrete foundation of specific values, beliefs and understandings that are listed in the handout I've just distributed. Let's review it point by point, and feel free to question and comment.**

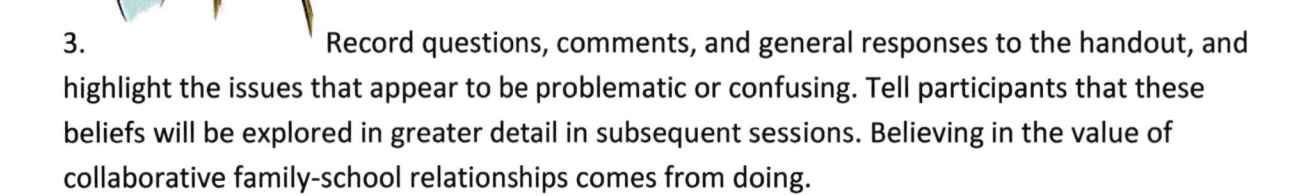

3. Record questions, comments, and general responses to the handout, and highlight the issues that appear to be problematic or confusing. Tell participants that these beliefs will be explored in greater detail in subsequent sessions. Believing in the value of collaborative family-school relationships comes from doing.

4. Say: **For example, it may be difficult to conceive of the benefits of a child being involved in meetings with parents and staff until one has actually participated in such a meeting. Has anyone had particular experiences that changed their views in any of the areas identified on the handout?**

5. Invite the participants to share their experiences with the group and to describe specifically what made the difference for them.

Activity III. Lecturette: Core Family-School Climate-Building Activities

INSTRUCTIONS

1. Say: **I'd like to give you an idea of the actual activities that create a collaborative climate. These are called Core Climate-Building Activities. They are activities that probably already exist in the school calendar and are restructured to become collaborative. There are four of these activities. Each of these will be the focus of several subsequent sessions, but it is important for you to get an overview before we actually learn more about each one.**

2. Distribute *Core Activities* Handout #2 and read through it with participants.

3. Invite participants to respond to the core activities and discuss how they think these would be received in their schools.

4. Distribute *Elective Activities* Handout #3 and read through it with participants.

5. Say: **In addition to core activities, many schools develop elective activities to address their unique needs or concerns. These can be classroom-based or school-wide. Examples of elective collaborative family-school climate-building activities are included in this handout.**

Activity IV. Fitting Collaboration into the Calendar

INSTRUCTIONS

1. **Say: It is often helpful for teachers and school personnel embarking on collaborative climate-building to see just how easily the core events we've discussed fit into the rhythm of the school year.**

   Let's use blank school calendars to consider when these events typically occur and how, taken together, they can send a strong and consistent signal that the school is committed to its relationships with families.

2. Distribute *Sample Academic Year Calendar* Handout #4.

3. Say: **Look at the school calendar and indicate in the appropriate month when events like orientations, multicultural night, parent-teacher conferences, and meetings for individual children who are having problems typically occur. Also, try to include any other activities that routinely engage or could include parents in your school. In later sessions, we will work more thoroughly to plan these events. For now, take the opportunity to look through the calendar and reflect on what is already in place in your school.**

Give time for participants to complete the calendars.

4. Say: **Could these events be made more collaborative? What message would it send to the families if they were? It would give signals throughout the school year that collaboration between family and school is how the school works routinely. Participation in these activities contributes to establishing a genuine partnership in support of the children's learning. Let's consider some examples of the how the timing of core activities can maximize their impact:**

   For example: (Choose one or two of the following examples, and paraphrase. Focus on how strategic timing is crucial in planning for long-term collaborative activities).

- A *Needs Assessment* could be conducted in the spring and planning for the coming year could begin with the sharing of the needs assessment results.

- *Family-School Orientations* in the early fall might be a new way of opening the school doors to families, informing them of the school's central belief about learning and teaching, giving examples of curriculum themes and setting a tone of collaboration. A consistent message can be communicated about how much the school values the family-school relationship as a central resource for student achievement and growth.

- *Family-Teacher Conferences* would occur in the late fall and again in the spring demonstrating the cumulative benefits of the family and school working closely together with the child. The students, parents and teacher(s) can share goals and address specific concerns.

- *Family-School Problem-Solving Meetings* are held throughout the year but may cluster around report card time and the end of the year when placement decisions are pending. Early in the school year, meetings can be convened to plan for the continued success of students who benefited from the collaborative process during the previous year. These meetings provide an on-going vehicle for experiencing the power of family-school collaboration and become a reminder that there is an effective way for families and schools to work together around even the most difficult problems.

SESSION 4
Handout 1

Basic Premises of Family-School Collaboration

Underlying collaborative climates are basic premises that derive from basic beliefs. These assumptions include:

- The *child* needs to be included as an active participant and decision-maker in family-school activities and in his/her educational experience in general.

- All individuals have been doing the best that they can under the circumstances. A *non-blaming atmosphere* is most effective for problem solving.

- All meetings can *result in a plan* in which every participant has a role.

- The school staff members, the children, and their families have *many available resources* that can be arranged together to make children's educational experiences stimulating and productive.

- *Parents care* about their children's education and their well-being.

- *School staff cares* about children's educational experiences and educational accomplishments.

- Educators, parents and children can restructure existing activities to *build in opportunities that enhance collaboration* and relationship building.

- Positive family-school interactions, activities, and events generate a *multiplier effect* that influences other aspects of the home and school life. Gradually, collaboration becomes the way of doing business in school. It becomes the norm rather than the exception.

- Families who are not able to attend family-school activities can *still feel included* and informed.

SESSION 4
Handout 2

Core Activities

- **The Collaborative Needs Assessment** - After administering a school climate questionnaire, school staff, parents/guardians, and possibly students analyze results and jointly determine what issues and areas need to be addressed. They assess the nature and level of collaboration which currently exists in their school and indicate the types and level of collaboration they would like to see exist.

- **Orientations** - Traditional "Meet the Teacher" events become Family-Teacher Orientations in which the children are included as active participants. There is a genuine three-way discussion among the teacher, the family and the students. Goals for the year are discussed. Additionally, curricular content and teaching strategies are demonstrated by engaging the students and their parents/guardians in collaborative activities. The school uses family-school orientations to send a clear and consistent message to students and their families that the family-school relationship is valued as a critical resource for maximizing student achievement. Parents/guardians learn how they can become productively involved to help their own children succeed.

- **Family-Teacher Conferences** - The Parent-Teacher Conference scheduled for daytime or evening hours is transformed into a Family-Teacher Meeting, which includes the student as an active participant. The child is prepared during classroom time to be an active participant. For example, students might first have an opportunity to assess their individual academic progress. They would identify their strengths and areas in need of improvement. They might role-play a meeting in which students, parents, and teacher discuss grades, strengths and weaknesses. They also make invitations to the conferences for their parents. Then, in the family-teacher meeting, the student shares in the discussion about his/her strengths and areas in need of improvement. Together the family, child and teacher determine a plan for meeting the child's needs.

- **Family-School Problem-Solving Meetings** - When a child is having social, emotional, academic and/or behavioral difficulties in school, the child, the parents/guardians and other family members, the teacher, and other relevant adults in the child's school life meet to share their concerns, reach consensus about what problem to work on, and jointly develop a concrete plan for solving the problem. This approach to problem solving is especially effective because it establishes a safe, non-blaming context where common goals and concerns about the child are emphasized and feasible solutions developed. Over time, children, staff and parents come to view these meetings, especially the inclusion of the child, as a natural way to solve problems. A critical outcome of these meetings is a shift in the relationship of family and school from distant (even adversarial) to collaborative. The collaborative process of the meeting and the plan becomes a model for subsequent interactions between family and school.

SESSION 4
Handout 3

Examples of Elective Collaborative Family-School Climate-Building Activities

- **Safety on the Bus** - Meeting with bus drivers, parents, teachers and children to improve behavior and cooperation on the bus.

- **Family-Reading** - A reading program which creatively engages children and parents/guardians in using reading skills at home in a range of situations, e.g., cooking, shopping, and talking about feelings.

- **Group Meeting for Students at Risk of Non-Promotion** - Meeting with groups of students, parents and teachers on each grade level to recognize strengths, identify areas for improvement, and create plans to improve performance in order to prevent students from being held-over.

- **Multicultural Night** - School-wide events to recognize and celebrate cultural/ethnic diversity, collaborative family-school activities like sharing international foods, singing songs from many countries, classroom-learning tasks related to culture (such as family stories, poetry and history illustrated by family trees) which promote family participation and sharing.

- **Grade-to-Grade Articulation Events** - Graduating students, their parents and teachers meet together to review accomplishments and to discuss what the students want their legacy to the school to be. Families, students, and teachers describe what they hope each graduating student will be doing ten years from that day. A similar event is held for students who will become the oldest or senior class to highlight and discuss the rights and responsibilities they will have as the new senior class.

SESSION 4
Handout 4

Sample Academic Year Calendar

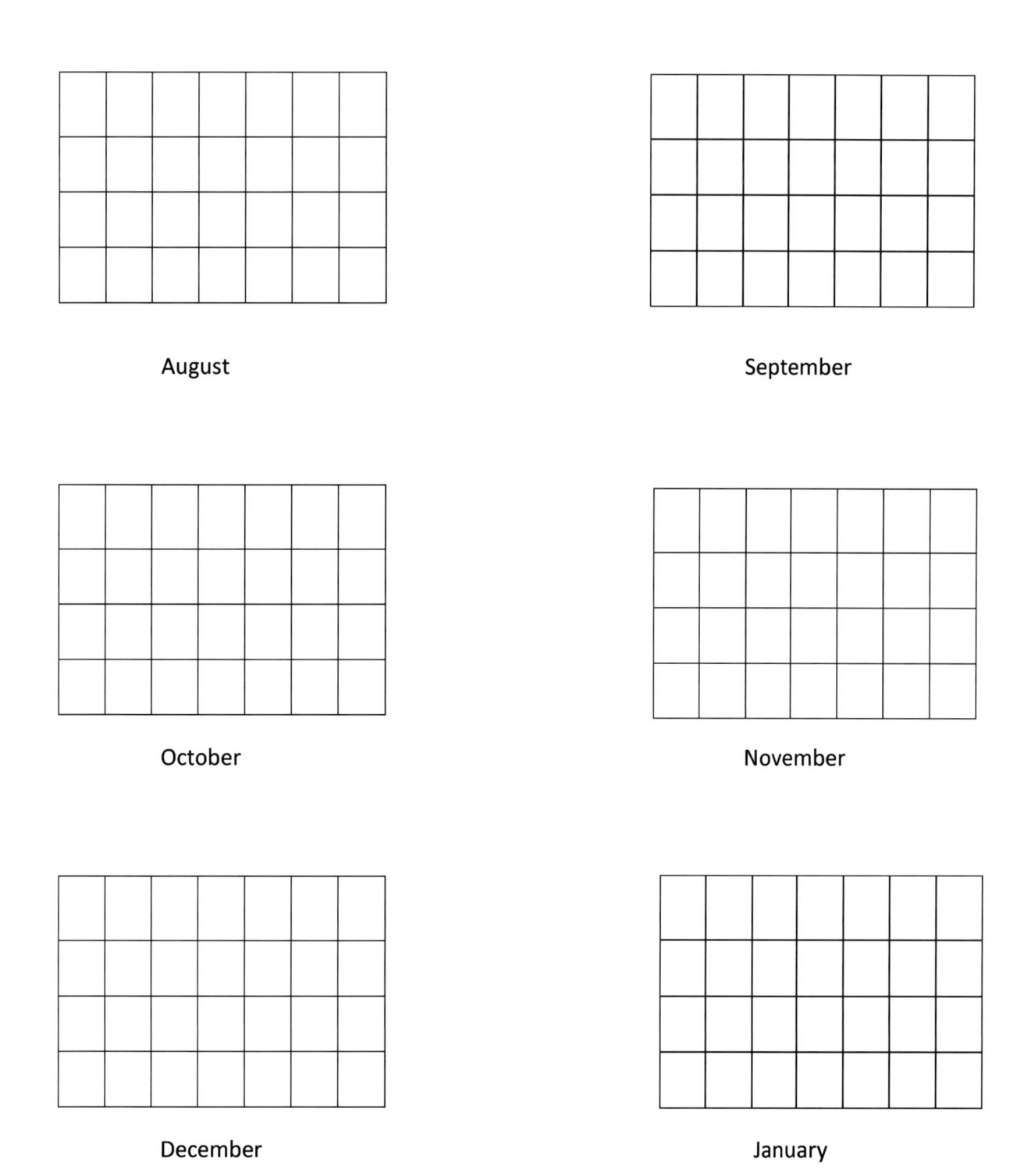

August

September

October

November

December

January

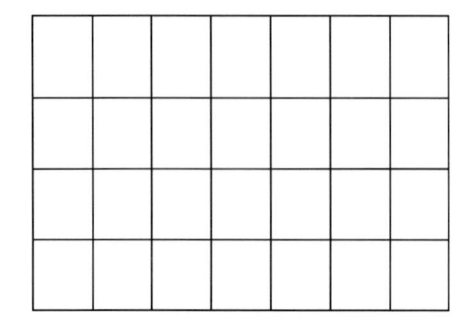

February

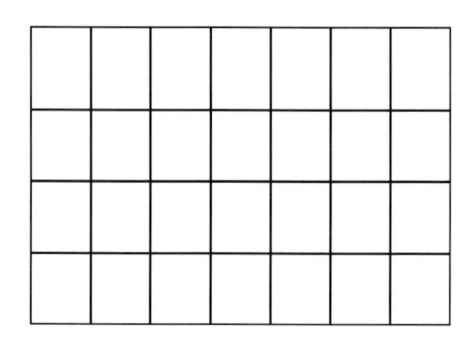

March

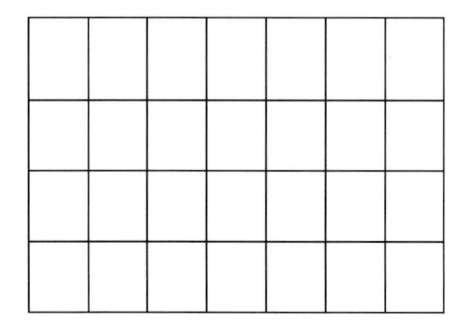

April

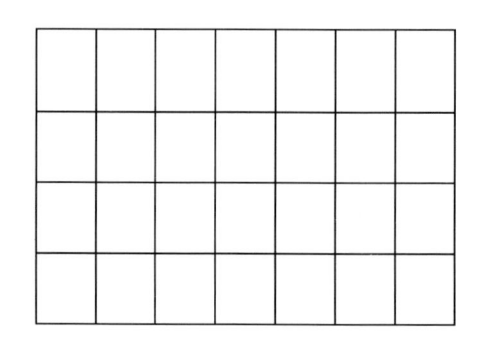

May

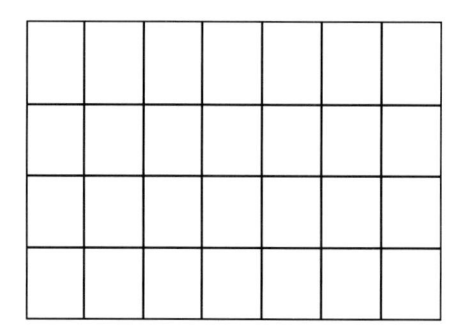

June

End of Session 4

SECTION 2

NEEDS ASSESSMENT: GETTING STARTED

SESSION 5: What are the benefits of a needs assessment, and how is data collected?

Rationale:

For many school personnel, presentation and distribution of needs assessments instruments are their first encounter with the prospect of family-school collaboration. Not only are staff members hearing a new and probably somewhat threatening idea, but also they are being asked to undertake yet another task- the completion of a survey. Thus even if school staff members do not yet grasp the uniqueness of this change effort and its possible value to them, they should have a clear idea of what they are being asked to do and why.

The goals of the needs assessment process as a whole can be summarized as follows:

1. To present the needs assessment to staff members in the clearest and least threatening way possible.

2. To encourage staff to understand the importance of participation for two key reasons: a) to provide a valid and meaningful beginning point for the change effort and b) to provide baseline data for ongoing assessment.

3. To use the teacher, family and student questionnaires as data collection tools.

4. To collect needs assessment data from teachers, school support staff, administrative staff, other school support staff, parents and/or students.

Goals
- To understand the first stage of the needs assessment process.
- To reflect on how the needs assessment process sets the tone for collaboration.
- To discuss how schools begin the data collection process.

Handouts/Materials
- *Family-School Climate Questionnaire: Teachers*
- *Family-School Climate Questionnaire: Families*
- *Family-School Climate Questionnaire: Middle and High School Students & Responses*
- White board/Smart Board or chart paper

Activity I. Looking at Your School

INSTRUCTIONS

1. **Say: In this and the next session we are going to begin the step-by-step process of determining what, if anything, you think most needs to change to create family-school collaboration in your school. With a questionnaire designed to assess your school's needs you will discover:**
   - **How people currently view the school**
   - **What concerns they have and what issues need to be addressed regarding family-school collaboration and**
   - **How people would like the school to be in the future.**

   The first step in the process aims:
   - **To find out how people currently view the school**
   - **To understand what concerns they have and what issues need to be addressed regarding family-school collaboration**
   - **To determine how they might like the school to be in the future.**

> *It may be helpful to anticipate some frequently asked questions about needs assessments.*
>
> **Q: Will We Ever Hear The Results Of These Surveys?**
>   A: Yes, the primary purpose of collecting this information is to share it as a tool for change. The results will be presented to school personnel and families so they can identify issues to work on.
>
> **Q: I Don't Have Enough Time To Do My Job Already. How Can I Be Expected To Fill Out More Forms?**
>   A: We understand how busy you are, but family-school collaboration is a high priority.
>
> **Q: How Much Time Will It Take To Complete This Questionnaire?**
>   A: 20-30 minutes

2. Discuss the procedures for administering the teacher, family and/or student questionnaires. The procedures can be explained in a variety of ways. One possibility is to appoint a point

person for the surveys, a member of the family-school team who makes copies of the questionnaire for all teachers and/or families (and middle or high school students), distributes the questionnaires, explains the purpose of needs assessment, answers individual questions and collects all the questionnaires upon completion.

In our experience, distributing, completing and collecting the questionnaires at a staff meeting where everyone is present is the most effective and efficient procedure for accomplishing this task.

3. Say: **Let's fill out an assessment questionnaire so that you have direct experience with the items. We can also use our group's data as a sample to analyze the results.**

4. Distribute *Climate Questionnaire: School Personnel* Handout #1. Instruct participants to fill out the questionnaire.

5. *Think About It*. Have participants reflect on the following:

- *What thoughts did you have as you filled out this survey questionnaire?*
- *What can the school learn from the data?*
- *What do you think the school could do with this data?*

6. Distribute *Climate Questionnaire: Families and Guardians* Handout #2 and *Middle and High School Students* Handout #3.

7. Say: **Now that we've experienced what it feels like to fill out a climate questionnaire ourselves, before the next session please distribute copies of the appropriate questionnaire to teachers at your school, families, and the students themselves. Please bring all the completed questionnaires to the next session for us to analyze together.**

SESSION 5
Handout 1

Family-School Climate Questionnaire: For School Personnel

Dear Teacher, Support Person, or Staff Member:

Please complete this questionnaire. Your answers will help us improve our school. We will learn more about how you currently see the school and what issues concern you.

Your answers will be strictly confidential.

Name (optional): _____   Date: _____

School: _____

What are **two issues facing the school** that you think are most important to address? For example: children learning to read, bullying, low morale. Please say briefly why you think each is a priority issue:

Issue #1: _____

Why? _____

_____

Issue #2: _____

Why? _____

_____

Describe a **strength of the school** that you think could be helpful in addressing the issues described above?

Strength: _____

_____

Please answer Questions 1-13 by putting in the left margin the number to reflect how you think things in the school *actually are.* If something is not applicable, please put NA.

How things **actually are:**
- 1 = almost never
- 2 = just a little
- 3 = somewhat
- 4 = usually
- 5 = almost all the time

_____1. The school is a welcoming place for families (i.e., entry signs, ways that office and/or security staff greet parents).

_____2. Examples of children's work are displayed in the hallways and classroom.

_____3. I assign family-oriented classroom assignments (e.g., family trees, family stories, recollection of historical events).

_____4. I let families know their child's strengths and accomplishments.

_____5. I can discuss children's challenges with their families without feeling that they'll blame me or my teaching.

_____6. I let families know right away if their child has a problem in school.

_____7. I conduct an orientation or "Meet the Teacher" meeting for the families of my class.

_____8. At least part of the orientation is held in my classroom so families can talk directly with me.

_____9. The children in my class attend the orientation meeting.

_____10. I feel comfortable having children attend their individual conferences with their families.

_____11. It is easy to find opportunities for families and teachers to communicate about students.

_____12. I welcome families' ideas and suggestions about how to help their child do well in school.

_____13. I know how to prepare children to participate in orientations and individual academic conferences with their families.

SESSION 5
Handout 2

Family-School Climate Questionnaire: For Families and Guardians

Dear Family Member or Guardian:

Please complete this questionnaire. Your answers will help us improve our school. We will learn more about how you currently see the school and what issues concern you.

Your answers will be strictly confidential.

Name (optional): _____   Date: _____

School: _____

What are **two issues facing the school** that you think are most important to address? For example: children learning to read, bullying, low morale. Please say briefly why you think each is a priority issue:

Issue #1: _____

Why? _____

_____

Issue #2: _____

Why? _____

_____

Describe a **strength of the school** that you think could be helpful in addressing the issues described above?

Strength: _____

_____

Please answer Questions 1-12 by putting in the left margin the number to reflect how you think things in the school *actually are.* If something is not applicable, please put NA.

How things **actually are**
   1 = almost never
   2 = just a little
   3 = somewhat
   4 = usually
   5 = almost all the time

_____1. The school is a welcoming place for families (i.e., entry signs, ways that office and/or security staff greet families).

_____2. Examples of children's work are displayed in the hallways and classroom.

_____3. My child's teacher assigns family-oriented classroom assignments (e.g., family trees, family stories, recollection of historical events).

_____4. My child's teacher lets me know about my child's strengths and accomplishments.

_____5. I can discuss my child's challenges with the teacher without feeling that they'll blame me.

_____6. The teacher lets me know right away if my child has a problem in school.

_____7. The school has an orientation or "Meet the Teacher" meeting for my child's class.

_____8. At least part of the orientation is held in the classroom so we can talk directly with our child's teacher.

_____9. My child attends the orientation meeting.

_____10. My child attends their individual conferences with me.

_____11. It is easy to find opportunities for families and teachers to communicate about students.

_____12. The teachers welcome my ideas and suggestions about how to help my child do well in school.

SESSION 5
Handout 3

Family-School Climate Questionnaire: For Middle and High School Students

Dear Students:

Please complete this questionnaire. Your answers will help us improve our school. We will learn more about how you currently see the school and what issues concern you.

Your answers will be strictly confidential.

Name (optional): _____ Date: _____

School: _____

What are **the two issues facing the school** that you think are most important to address? For example: college readiness, graduating on time, bullying. Please say briefly why you think each is a priority issue:

Issue #1:_____

Why?_____

_____

Issue #2:_____

Why? _____

_____

Describe a **strength of the school** that you think could be helpful in addressing the issues described above?

Strength: _____

_____

_____

Please answer Questions 1-13 by putting in the left margin the number to reflect how you think things in the school *actually are.* If something is not applicable, please put NA.

How things **actually are**
    1 = almost never
    2 = just a little
    3 = somewhat
    4 = usually
    5 = almost all the time

_____1. The school is a welcoming place for students and their families (i.e., entry signs, ways that office and/or security staff greet parents).

_____2. Examples of my work and my classmates' work are displayed in the hallways and classroom.

_____3. My teachers assign family-oriented classroom assignments (e.g., family trees, family stories, recollection of historical events).

_____4. My teachers let me and my family know my strengths and accomplishments.

_____5. I can discuss my challenges with my teachers without feeling blamed.

_____6. After they've talked to me, my teachers let my family know right away if I'm having a problem in school.

_____7. The school has an orientation or "Meet the Teacher" meeting for my class.

_____8. At least part of the orientation is held in my classrooms so my family can talk directly with my teachers.

_____9. I am invited to attend the orientation meeting.

_____10. My teachers help me prepare for orientations and individual academic conferences with my family.

_____11. I feel comfortable attending my individual conferences with my teachers and my family.

_____12. It is easy to find opportunities to talk with my teachers about my progress in school.

_____13. The teachers welcome my ideas and suggestions about how I can improve in school.

End of Session 5

SESSION 6: How do we use the results of the needs assessments to shape our decision-making processes?

Rationale:

The delivery of feedback of the questionnaire results to the school staff is an important part of the needs assessment process. At this point staff members can realize the benefits of having taken the time and energy to complete the questionnaires. They have an opportunity to review the results, see their school from a different perspective and begin to plan for change.

It is also critical that the results are provided in a very user-friendly and understandable way to promote collaboration and enthusiasm towards next steps in the change process. Once staff members are able to interact with and ponder the implications of the results, they begin to feel a sense of ownership in the information and the change process. Rather than merely being informed of the results, they are asked to work collaboratively to bring their experience in the school to the data analysis process.

Goals:

- To begin analyzing survey data.
- To explore meaningful ways to present data results to staff and parents.
- To actively determine priorities for change in participants' schools using survey results.

Handouts/Materials:

- Family-School Climate Questionnaire (one used last session)
- Family-School Climate Questionnaire RESULTS FORM for Teachers
- Family-School Climate Questionnaire RESULTS FORM for Families
- Family-School Climate Questionnaire RESULTS FORM for Middle and High School Students
- Data Analysis
- Data Tally Sheet
- White board/Smart Board or chart paper

Introduction

Say: **Today we are going to have the opportunity to review and interpret the needs assessment data we collected. We're going to use the Questionnaire for School Personnel that you've distributed in your own schools. As you compare these results with** your experiences, you will be able to use these findings to suggest directions for change. After this session, you'll be able to analyze the data from the other questionnaires on your own.

Activity I. Tallying Data

INSTRUCTIONS

1. Distribute *Data Analysis* Handout #4 and *Family-School Climate Questionnaire: School Personnel Response Form* Handout #3 to participants.

2. Explain to participants that we are going to tally the data in accordance with the *Data Analysis* handout.

3. Distribute *Data Tally Sheet* Handout #5.

4. Instruct them to break into small groups of 4 or 5 people. Make sure that the Results Forms for each constituency who completed the questionnaires - the families, school personnel and, if relevant, middle and high school students - are distributed evenly across groups, one to a group.

5. Explain that in their groups they are to circle all of scores that are *below a mean of 2.0 and above a mean of 4.0* in order to further analyze the data results. Allot 10-15 minutes for this exercise. Once they have completed that task, they should review the issues that emerged as most pressing for the group whose Results Form they are analyzing.

Activity II. Identifying Themes

INSTRUCTIONS

1. Once the groups have identified all the scores below 2.0 and above 4.0, ask them to review both the issues which respondents cited as most pressing and those that emerge both within and between the high and low score clusters. Groups should be prepared to summarize these themes or issues. For example, groups may find low scores on parent ease in discussing their child's difficulties, but may also find high scores for families saying a key issue for them is having more open access to their children's teachers. This may represent their awareness of the gap between what currently exists and what families hope will develop.

2. Say: **Once you have discussed the themes and/or issues which you see emerging, I'd like each group to identify and record the two issues which you think must be addressed as well as the school strength that could help create a more collaborative family-school climate. Let's have one member of the group report your findings to the large group.**

3. Record these issues on the writing board or chart paper.

4. Explain that the reason for doing this is to use the results of the needs assessment as a basis for planning activities.

Activity III. Wrap-Up

INSTRUCTIONS

1. Referring to the writing board or chart paper, lead a discussion comparing, contrasting and elaborating on issues presented by the groups. At the conclusion of the discussion, the entire group should identify the two or three issues they would most like to address through a school-wide or classroom focused family-school activity and the school strengths that could help achieve this. Circle these on the board or add/paraphrase them at the bottom.

2. Tell participants that next session, we will expand our knowledge about how to solve these problems collaboratively.

SESSION 6
Handout 1

Family-School Climate Questionnaire RESULTS FORM
For School Personnel

Here are the two issues school personnel at our school cited as most pressing.

Issue #1:_____

citing this issue _____

Issue #2:_____

citing this issue _____

Other issues cited:_____

_____

Here is a strength school personnel at our school cited as most helpful.

Strength:_____

citing this strength _____

Other strengths cited:_____

_____

How things **actually are**
1 = almost never
2 = just a little
3 = somewhat
4 = usually
5 = almost all the time

In the blanks next to each question please transfer the average score for each question from the Tally Sheet.

_____1. The school is a welcoming place for families (i.e., entry signs, ways that office and/or security staff greet parents).

_____2. Examples of children's work are displayed in the hallways and classroom.

_____3. I assign family-oriented classroom assignments (e.g., family trees, family stories, recollection of historical events).

_____4. I let families know their child's strengths and accomplishments.

_____5. I can discuss children's challenges with their families without feeling that they'll blame me or my teaching.

_____6. I let families know right away if their child has a problem in school.

_____7. I conduct an orientation or "Meet the Teacher" meeting for the families of my class.

_____8. At least part of the orientation is held in my classroom so families can talk directly with me.

_____9. The children in my class attend the orientation meeting.

_____10. I feel comfortable having children attend their individual conferences with their families.

_____11. It is easy to find opportunities for families and teachers to communicate about students.

_____12. I welcome families' ideas and suggestions about how to help their child do well in school.

_____13. I know how to prepare children to participate in orientations and individual academic conferences with their families.

SESSION 6
Handout 2

Family-School Climate Questionnaire RESULTS FORM
For Families and Guardians

Here are the two issues families and guardians at our school cited as most pressing.

Issue #1:_____

citing this issue _____

Issue #2:_____

citing this issue _____

Other issues cited:_____

_____

Here is a strength families and guardians at our school cited as most helpful.

Strength:_____

citing this strength _____

Other strengths cited:_____

_____

How things **actually are**
1 = almost never
2 = just a little
3 = somewhat
4 = usually
5 = almost all the time

In the blanks next to each question please transfer the average score for each question from the Tally Sheet.

_____1. The school is a welcoming place for families (i.e., entry signs, ways that office and/or security staff greet parents).

_____2. Examples of children's work are displayed in the hallways and classroom.

_____3. My child's teacher assigns family-oriented classroom assignments (e.g., family trees, family stories, recollection of historical events).

_____4. My child's teacher lets me know about my child's strengths and accomplishments.

_____5. I can discuss my child's challenges with the teacher without feeling that they'll blame me.

_____6. The teacher lets me know right away if my child has a problem in school.

_____7. The school has an orientation or "Meet the Teacher" meeting for my child's class.

_____8. At least part of the orientation is held in the classroom so we can talk directly with our child's teacher.

_____9. My child attends the orientation meeting.

_____10. My child attends their individual conferences with me.

_____11. It is easy to find opportunities for families and teachers to communicate about students.

_____12. The teachers welcome my ideas and suggestions about how to help my child do well in school.

SESSION 6
Handout 3

Family-School Climate Questionnaire RESULTS FORM
For Middle and High School Students

Here are the two issues students at our school cited as most pressing.

Issue #1:_____

citing this issue _____

Issue #2:_____

citing this issue _____

Other issues cited:_____

_____

Here is a strength students at our school cited as most helpful.

Strength:_____

citing this strength _____

Other strengths cited:_____

_____

How things **actually are**
1 = almost never
2 = just a little
3 = somewhat
4 = usually
5 = almost all the time

In the blanks next to each question please transfer the average score for each question from the Tally Sheet.

_____1. The school is a welcoming place for students and their families (i.e., entry signs, ways that office and/or security staff greet families).

_____2. Examples of my work and my classmates' work are displayed in the hallways and classroom.

_____3. My teachers assign family-oriented classroom assignments (e.g., family trees, family stories, recollection of historical events).

_____4. My teachers let me and my family know my strengths and accomplishments.

_____5. I can discuss my challenges with my teachers without feeling blamed.

_____6. After they've talked to me, my teachers let my family know right away if I'm having a problem in school.

_____7. The school has an orientation or "Meet the Teacher" meeting for my class.

_____8. At least part of the orientation is held in my classrooms so my family can talk directly with my teachers.

_____9. I am invited to attend the orientation meeting.

_____10. My teachers help me prepare for orientations and individual academic conferences with my family.

_____11. I feel comfortable attending my individual conferences with my teachers and my family.

_____12. It is easy to find opportunities to talk with my teachers about my progress in school.

_____13. The teachers welcome my ideas and suggestions about how I can improve in school.

SESSION 6
Handout 4

Data Analysis

INSTRUCTIONS

1. Summarizing the data may seem to be a complex task. However, if you follow the instructions below using the Data Analysis Tally Sheet, you will find that it will be manageable. Plan to spend 3-5 hours analyzing the data.

2. In order to understand how many people responded and what their responses to each question were, it is probably best to analyze the questionnaires one question at a time. For each question, using the data tally response sheet, you will learn how many people chose each rating. Now beginning with question #1, go through all of the questionnaires and for each one make a mark (tick) in the tally sheet under the rating that corresponds to the one chosen by the respondent.

3. For each question, add up the total number of responses for each possible choice. Write this total on the tally sheet (i.e., | | | |... This equals 4 responses).

4. Add these totals across to determine the total number of people who completed that question. This total will be referred to as A. (i.e., A or the total number of responses (frequency) is 12 + 9 +4+ 10 =35).

5. Multiply the total number of responses for each possible rating by that rating. Then sum all of these totals. This total will be referred to as B.
(i.e., 12 responses for a rating of 1 is 12 * 1 = 12; 9 responses for the rating of 2 is 9 * 2 = 18; 4 responses for a rating of 3 is 4 * 3 = 12; and 10 responses for a rating of 4 is 10 * 4 = 40). B or the grand total is 12+ 18+ 12+40=82.

6. Then divide B or the grand total by A the frequency of responses to get the mean score or average score for each question (B/A or 82/35 = 2.3).

7. Now you have the average or mean score for each question. In order to discuss the findings with the staff and families, it would be helpful to list all of the mean or average scores for each question on a blank copy of the Family-School Climate Questionnaire (see Family-School Climate Questionnaire RESULTS FORMS for Families, Teachers and Students in Session 6).

SESSION 6
Handout 5

Data Tally Sheet

Version: (circle one)

      School Personnel   Families/Guardians   Middle and High School Students

"What are the two issues facing the school that you think are most important to address?"

DIRECTIONS: Go through all of the completed questionnaires and list in the appropriate spaces below what each respondent listed as 1st and 2nd priority issues. When an issue first appears, list it and put a tick (tally mark, I) next to it. Each time it reappears do not re-list it. Instead put an additional tick next to it. This will indicate that it's been chosen more than once. [Read through without tabulating the "why" portion of these questions to gain a deeper understanding of what factors respondents think create the issue.]

Example:

Issue #1:

Issue Name	Tally
Improving school discipline	IIIII IIIII IIIII
Giving parents a say in their children's learning	IIIII IIIII
Getting help with homework	IIIII III
Safety on the playground	II

Issue #1:

Issue Name	Tally

Issue #2:

Issue Name	Tally

Strength:

Strength Name	Tally

Once you've listed ALL of the issues cited by each respondent, count the total number of times all issues were cited as a 1st priority and then indicate the # of times each issue was listed as #1 priority from highest to lowest times cited. For example, if the total # of citations under Issue #1 is 35, and safety on the playground is cited 2 times, giving parents a say in their children's learning is cited 10 times, getting help with homework is listed 8 times and improving school discipline is listed 15 times, then you would list them in the following order:

Issue # 1 – total # of choices – 35

```
Improving school discipline: 15
Giving parents a say in their children's learning: 10
Getting help with homework: 8
Safety on the playground: 2
```

Repeat this process for Issue #2 and for the Strength.

Issue #1:

Issue #2:

Strength:

Closed-Ended Questions

For each respondent, tally the # chosen for each question below that question.

Example:

_____1. The school is a welcoming place for parents (i.e., entry signs, ways that office and/or security staff greet parents).

1 |||
2 |||||||||
3 ||||||||||
4 ||||||||
5 |||||

_____2. Examples of children's work *(my work and my classmates' work)* are displayed in the hallways and classroom.

1 _____
2 _____
3 _____
4 _____
5 _____

_____3. I *(my child's teacher/my teachers)* assign family-oriented classroom assignments (e.g., family trees, family stories, recollection of historical events).

1 _____
2 _____
3 _____
4 _____
5 _____

_____4. I *(My child's teacher/my teachers)* let families *(me/my family)* know their child's *(my)* strengths and accomplishments.

1 _____
2 _____
3 _____
4 _____
5 _____

_____5. I can discuss children's *(my child's/my)* challenges with their families *(my child's teacher/my teachers)* without feeling blamed.

1 _____
2 _____
3 _____
4 _____
5 _____

_____6. I let parents/guardians know right away if their child has a problem in school *(My child's teacher lets me know right away if my child has a problem in school/After they've talked to me, my teachers let my family know right away if I'm having a problem in school)*.

1 _____
2 _____
3 _____
4 _____
5 _____

_____7. I conduct an orientation or "Meet the Teacher" meeting for the families of my class *(The school has an orientation or "Meet the Teacher" meeting for my child's/my class)*.

1 _____
2 _____
3 _____
4 _____
5 _____

_____8. At least part of the orientation is held in my classroom so parents*(we)* can talk directly with me *(our child's teacher/my teachers)*.

1 _____
2 _____
3 _____
4 _____
5 _____

_____9. The children in my class *(My child)* attend*(s)* the orientation meeting/*(I am invited to attend the orientation meeting)*.

1 _____
2 _____
3 _____
4 _____
5 _____

_____10. I feel comfortable having children attend *(my child attends/I feel comfortable attending)* their *(my)* individual conferences with their families *(me)*.

1 _____
2 _____
3 _____
4 _____
5 _____

_____11. It is easy to find opportunities for parents and teachers to communicate about students *(to talk with my teachers about my progress in school)*.

1 _____
2 _____
3 _____
4 _____
5 _____

_____12. I *(The teachers)* welcome parents'/guardians' *(my)* ideas and suggestions about how to help their *(my)* child *(me)* do well in school.

1 _____
2 _____
3 _____
4 _____
5 _____

_____13. I know how to prepare children *(My teachers help prepare me)* to participate in orientations and individual academic conferences with their *(my)* families.

1 _____
2 _____
3 _____
4 _____
5 _____

End of Session 6

SECTION 3

THE COLLABORATIVE APPROACH: THE MEETING FLOW STEPS

I. The Collaborative Process

SESSION 7: How can we prepare for the realities of family-school collaboration?

Rationale:

One of the central goals of collaboration is to include **every family** in their child's school experience in an educationally meaningful way. In this way, we can work together to build genuine partnerships between family and school, which foster:

- Prevention and early detection of learning and social issues,
- Celebration of students' accomplishments and their family backgrounds, and
- Intervention when problems do arise.

Through collaboration, we seek to help families and schools increase the ways they communicate with each other in order to promote students' success in school. Built on a foundation of respectful and non-blaming interaction, a collaborative approach hinges on the inclusion of the child in all collaborative efforts between these two systems. In this session we introduce an approach to problem solving which is central to creating productive and hopeful conversations between families and schools.

Goals

- To articulate examples and characteristics of collaborative problem solving.
- To reflect on the value of, and possible issues related to, including the child in collaborative problem solving meetings.
- To assess school readiness for implementation of further collaboration.

Handouts/Materials

- *Vignettes of Collaborative Problem-Solving I: Lisette* and *II: Bus Riders*
- *School Readiness for Collaboration*
- White board/Smart Board or chart paper

Introduction

Say: **Today we are going to introduce an approach to problem solving which is central to creating productive and hopeful conversations between families and** schools. We will begin by exploring ways to address the most pressing issues in your school with collaborative problem-solving techniques. Today, we'll discuss the benefits of this approach and think about its application in your school.

Activity I. Vignettes of Collaborative Problem-Solving

INSTRUCTIONS

1. Distribute *Vignettes of Collaborative Problem-Solving I: Lisette* Handout #1 and *Vignettes of Collaborative Problem-Solving II: Bus Riders* Handout #2. Read the top portion on each handout, not the collaborative solution (yet). After reading the description, ask the group how a school would traditionally handle the problem.

2. List responses on divided writing board or chart paper under the headings Problem 1 and Problem 2.

3. After participants have described typical, traditional attempts to solve these problems, explain that we are going to explore collaborative approaches to each one of these actual situations.

4. Ask participants to read the collaborative solutions. After participants have heard/read the collaborative solutions to these problems, ask them how these solutions compare with those previously listed as traditional solutions. Invite them to share their reactions to the collaborative vignettes.

Activity II. Elements of Collaboration

INSTRUCTIONS

1. Say: **Based on the handout and our discussions of collaboration thus far, what are the elements of each of the two vignettes we've discussed that make them collaborative?**

2. List participants' responses.

3. Say: **What do you see as the chief benefits of collaborative problem solving for each of the participants, i.e. the family, the child, the school?**

4. Ask participants to compare the traditional and collaborative solutions in terms of how the participants in each situation would feel and benefit as a result of each.

5. Divide them into small groups. Assign each group a point of view, i.e. the parents, school personnel, students, bus drivers, from which they are to discuss participants' reactions to the traditional vs. the collaborative solution.

6. Have small groups report out. Record participants' responses in three columns labeled 1) families, 2) school personnel and school-related personnel and 3) students.

7. Summarize their responses and integrate the following into your summary if participants haven't mentioned them:

- Collaboration benefits the family by increasing access to information, expanding avenues of communication with school staff and empowering the family to play a more active role in the child's academic progress.

- It benefits the school by helping school staff hear the family's point of view in a non-blaming manner and by promoting a shared sense of responsibility between family and school in the education of each child.

- It benefits the child by actively involving him or her in the decision making process, thus promoting a sense of responsibility. By involving the child in collaborative meetings, children can join their parents and teachers and other school staff as they work together to constructively resolve a particular concern.

- Most importantly, the inclusion of the child in problem-solving meetings shifts the role of the child from message bearer or passive recipient of decisions to active participant in concerns relating to his or her own school progress.

Activity III. Including the Child

INSTRUCTIONS

1. Say: **One of the most significant aspects of our approach to family-school collaboration is the inclusion of the child in all meetings pertaining to him or her. While some educators are immediately comfortable with this idea, others are understandably concerned about its impact on the child and on the types of discussions adults can have in the child's presence.**

2. Say: **You now might see some advantages to having the child in the meeting, but I'm sure you may still see some difficulties as well. What problems do you foresee?**
Ask the participants for feedback. If the following are not mentioned, be sure to bring them up and summarize their possible solution:

> **PROBLEM 1:** *Child might be embarrassed or upset at bringing up family problems.*
>
> **SOLUTION:** Family problems are less likely to be the focus of the meeting if the child is there. The focus of these meetings ought to be the child's education. Moreover, if family problems are raised it may be doubtful that the child would really be embarrassed. If anything, the child might be relieved that someone knows about and is talking about the problem at home. Remember that there are no family secrets. The child is well aware of much of what goes on and bringing it out into the open could be very helpful to the child. If the parents really want to give you some information about the family that would be inappropriate for the child to hear, ask the child to step out at the end of the meeting because there is some adult information that needs to be shared.
>
> **PROBLEM 2:** *Saying negative things in front of the child is difficult.*
>
> **SOLUTION:** This may be alleviated if the child helps prepare for the meeting by listing out what he does well and what he has difficulty with. This gives the teacher a chance to emphasize what is going well. It also signals to the child that all children have trouble with some things and that is normal. Furthermore, it's no secret to the child that is doing poorly or needs improvement in something. If that can be discussed in a way that results in his getting some help or seeing some other ways to handle the situation, then the child might be relieved.
>
> **PROBLEM 3:** *The child might feel outnumbered.*
>
> **SOLUTION:** This again could be alleviated by preparing the child. Then the information has come from the child rather than from the teacher.

> **PROBLEM 4:** *Dealing with problems such as drug abuse or a bitter marital struggle in front of the child would be inappropriate.*
>
> **SOLUTION:** First, it's important to ask whether the discussion of these topics is an appropriate use of a teacher conference. It may be best to use the conference time to focus on what's best for the child rather than what's wrong with the parent. If these topics arise, acknowledge them by mentioning that they might be more appropriately addressed in a different forum – such as a problem-solving meeting – with mental health professionals present.
>
> **PROBLEM 5:** *There are too many children with difficult situations in my classroom for me to feel comfortable trying this.*
>
> **SOLUTION:** Don't try this with all of the children in your class. Select a few, at first. After you develop your skills in leading these meetings, there will be fewer and fewer issues and problems you will feel unable to handle.

We have found that there **are two exceptions to the principle of including the child**. First, we do not include the child in hostile marital or separation/divorce situations in which one or both parents indicate that they cannot be constructive with the other. It still may be useful to include the child in separate meetings with each parent, so that a clear, consistent and strong message about both parents' interest in the child's learning is communicated.

The second exception involves suspected child abuse situations in which state mandated procedures are to be followed. We will elaborate on ways to structure family-teacher meetings in a subsequent workshop.

Activity IV. School Readiness

INSTRUCTIONS

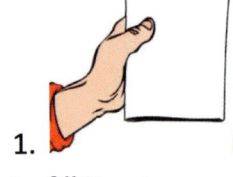

1. Distribute *School Readiness for Collaboration* Handout #3 and ask participants to fill it out.

2. On writing board or chart paper, list out participants' responses to questions 1 and 2. List question 1 under the title "Resources" and 2 under "Characteristics of Collaboration." After listing is completed, note the common elements in responses.

3. After discussing the common elements of responses for numbers 1 and 2, make a third column designated "Obstacles" and lead a discussion about these.

4. *Think About It.* Ask the participants to reflect upon the following:

- What has already been tried in your school to deal with the "obstacles?"

- What else do you think needs to be done to overcome these obstacles?

> **TIP!** If time permits, invite people from the same school or from schools with similar issues to get into small groups and brainstorm ways of overcoming obstacles to collaboration. Have participants record their ideas and suggest that each person or group of people identify one idea they will try to implement in their school.

SESSION 7
Handout 1

Vignettes of Collaborative Problem Solving I: Lisette

VIGNETTE 1

The Problem:

Lisette is a second grade student in an inner city elementary school. She lives with her mother, her grandmother and several cousins. She is a very good student although other children from her extended family have had numerous difficulties in school. The extended family has a history of unsuccessful interactions with the school. Her mother and father are in the process of getting a divorce and her grandfather to whom she was very close died recently. Mrs. Alvarez, Lisette's teacher, has noticed that she has become increasingly quiet and seems sad and withdrawn. Lisette has complained to the teacher that she dislikes the visitation agreement stipulating that she spends occasional weekends at her father's mother's house. In the last few weeks her schoolwork has been deteriorating. The teacher has discussed the problem with the guidance counselor.

The Collaborative Solution:

The guidance counselor convened and facilitated a family-school problem-solving meeting, which was attended by Lisette, her mother, and the teacher. As concerns were discussed, Lisette was able to explain that her sadness in class occurred when she thought about and missed her grandfather, and that her visits to her paternal grandmother's were not as upsetting to her right now. Lisette and her mother were able to cry together at the meeting -- something they had not done since the death. A plan was developed in which it was agreed that:

1. Lisette and her mother would spend time looking at pictures and talking or writing about her grandfather.

2. Lisette would bring a picture of her grandfather to school and with the teacher decide where in the classroom she would like to put it. She would be able to look at the picture whenever she missed her grandfather.

3. The family would begin counseling sessions at a local mental health facility with the goal of helping Lisette's parents deal more constructively with each other and reducing the amount of conflict to which Lisette was exposed.

4. The teacher would check in with Lisette periodically to see how she was doing and would encourage her to interact more with peers by creating an art project for her and a girl of her choice.

The teacher reported that within a few days Lisette's mood improved and she was more attentive, active and cheerful in the classroom.

SESSION 7
Handout 2

Vignettes of Collaborative Problem Solving II: Bus Riders

VIGNETTE 2

The Problem:

A small group of students who are bussed from a distant corner of the school district to an elementary school have been disruptive on the bus. There has been so much fighting, roughhousing and throwing of objects that the driver is seriously concerned about the children's safety. Calls made to their parents have not resulted in any improvement in the situation.

The Collaborative Solution:

The guidance counselor and the principal decided that it would be most effective to bring all of the parties together to air their concerns and find a meaningful solution to the problem. A problem-solving meeting was attended by the eight students, six of their parents, the bus driver, the guidance counselor, the principal and the Facilitator. After describing the purpose of the meeting and explaining that this was a non-blaming, non-punishment meeting, the Facilitator invited each person to share one or two key concerns about the bus situation. It became apparent that the students did not realize how dangerous their behavior was and were unclear about school bus rules. The driver had not understood the importance of clarifying and posting the school bus rules for the students nor had he responded with consequences to the misbehavior, e.g., if the students threw things out of the windows, then the bus windows would be closed for a day. Despite the calls they had received, most of the parents were unaware of the severity of the problem. Together the group identified solutions to the problem including:

1. Although parents could not act as bus monitors (because of insurance issues), they would monitor the students at bus stops. They intended to remind them of the bus rules before they boarded the bus and help them board the bus in an orderly fashion.

2. The driver agreed to review bus rules with the students and to post them in the bus to serve as a continual reminder of his expectations.

3. The driver and parents agreed to determine consequences for breaking rules.

4. Students agreed that if their behaviors did not improve bus seats would be assigned.

5. Parents set up a communication system among themselves and with the driver so they could establish regular contact. They exchanged phone numbers with each other and the driver and agreed to contact parents who were not at the meeting regarding the bus situations.

6. The school personnel agreed to communicate with the driver on a daily basis to monitor the situation and to keep parents informed.

7. The guidance counselor suggested that the group meet again in a few weeks to assess progress.

The guidance counselor reported that at the follow-up meeting all parties agreed that the situation had improved since the previous meeting.

SESSION 7
Handout 3

School Readiness for Collaborative Problem-Solving

1. List five characteristics or resources of your school that currently support a collaborative approach to problem-solving for individual students, classrooms or the entire school (e.g., active parent body, strong leadership by building principal, committed teachers, interested guidance counselor or school social worker, positive climate throughout school, community support, etc.).

   a. _____

   b. _____

   c. _____

   d. _____

   e. _____

2. What would *have to happen*– i.e. what would you have to actually see-- for you to assert unequivocally that problems were being solved collaboratively between families and your school?

   a. _____

   b. _____

   c. _____

   d. _____

   e. _____

3. What are some of the obstacles that make it difficult to develop collaborative problem solving in your school (e.g., overworked parents, lack of leadership, teachers focused on basics, little respect for parents, poor communications structures between home and school, negative school climate)?

   a. _____

   b. _____

End of Session 7

II. Finding Facts

SESSION 8: What is fact-finding, and how can interviewing skills help?

Rationale:

Developing a "tool kit" of micro and macro interviewing skills will enable educators to ask questions and obtain information clearly and concisely in their interactions in the classroom and in other group activities. It is essential to ask questions of students, parents and teachers in ways that establish a non-blaming and collaborative climate. Skillful questioning helps people respond appropriately and freely. These skills are particularly useful for working with others to explore critical issues and to resolve problems.

Goals

- To identify interviewing skills which can be used to promote collaborative communication and improve relationships.
- To understand and illustrate what function these skills serve.
- To apply macro and micro interviewing skills to help enhance knowledge of finding facts.

Handouts/Materials

- Collaborative Meeting Flow Steps: Finding Facts
- Finding Facts
- Micro Interviewing Skills
- Macro Interviewing Skills

Introduction

Whether you find yourself in a problem-solving meeting context or a routine conference, Finding Facts is a crucial part of the collaborative meeting. Finding facts in a non-blaming way requires familiarity with key interviewing skills. These tools provide effective ways of asking questions and responding to statements. They enable one to become a group leader or participant who can keep a discussion focused, maintain an appropriate pace, and enable participants to have their ideas heard and addressed.

Activity I. Introducing Finding Facts

INSTRUCTIONS

1. Distribute *Collaborative Meeting Flow Steps: Finding Facts* Handout #1.

2. Say: **These Meeting Flow Steps are the backbone of collaborative work in schools. Each one represents a different stage in a collaborative meeting. Let's go around the room and have each person read a step to give you an overview. We are going to explore each of these steps in depth throughout our sessions. Today, we're going to focus on the step entitled *Finding Facts*.**

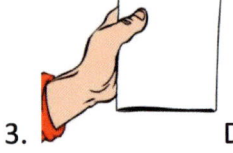

3. Distribute *Finding Facts* Handout #2. Read over with participants and ask for feedback.

Activity II. Role Play: Micro Interviewing Skills

INSTRUCTIONS

1. Distribute *Micro Interviewing Skills* Handout #3. Review examples and definitions in each set.

2. Distribute *Brianna Case Description* Handout #5.

3. Instruct participants to divide into groups of three with
   - **A as Teacher**
   - **B as Parent and**
   - **C as Child**

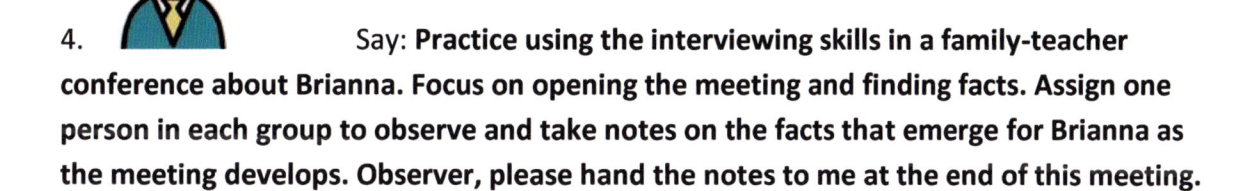

4. Say: **Practice using the interviewing skills in a family-teacher conference about Brianna. Focus on opening the meeting and finding facts. Assign one person in each group to observe and take notes on the facts that emerge for Brianna as the meeting develops. Observer, please hand the notes to me at the end of this meeting.**

5. After three minutes, ask participants to switch roles until each member has had a chance to practice the micro interviewing skills as the teacher, "A." Instruct participants that after each of the following role-play sequences, they should give each other feedback on the use of the specific micro interviewing skills they are applying:

   - In the first role-play, "A" should focus on *using 10 words or less* and *avoiding yes/no questions.*
   - In the second role-play, "A" should focus on *using 10 words or less, avoiding yes/no questions,* and *avoiding why questions.*
   - In the third role play, A should apply all 5 micro interviewing techniques: *using 10 words or less, avoiding yes/no questions, avoiding why questions, no double barreled questions* and *putting the verb first.*

6. *Think About It.* Ask participants to reflect on the following questions and report out to the group:

- *What was difficult about using these micro-interviewing skills?*

- *How did they enhance the interaction?*

Activity III. Role Play: Macro Interviewing Skills

INSTRUCTIONS

1. Distribute *Macro Interviewing Skills* Handout #4.

2. Ask participants to divide into groups of six with
   - **A as Administrator**
   - **B as Parent**
   - **C as Science Teacher**
   - **D and E as Students and**
   - **F as Group Facilitator**

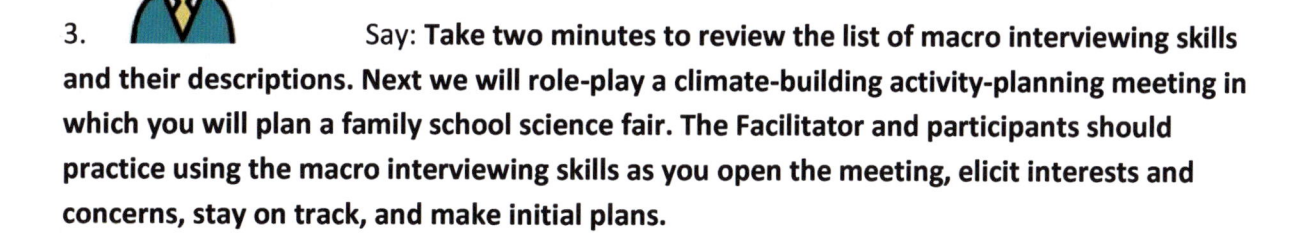

3. Say: **Take two minutes to review the list of macro interviewing skills and their descriptions. Next we will role-play a climate-building activity-planning meeting in which you will plan a family school science fair. The Facilitator and participants should practice using the macro interviewing skills as you open the meeting, elicit interests and concerns, stay on track, and make initial plans.**

4. *Think About It.* After participants have completed the role-play, reconvene the large group and discuss the following:

   - *How was a collaborative tone set in your planning meeting?*
   - *Which interviewing skills were used in the meeting?*
   - *How did the use of these interviewing skills contribute to effective problem solving?*

5. Say: **These skills look very simple as they're listed on the handout you received. However, they are very difficult to master. Usually it takes several years of practice before you can really have such control over these skills that you use them without thinking about it. It is important, therefore, to use them now self-consciously as often as possible. They can be used**

in conversations with students, class meetings, faculty meetings or phone calls to parents, or discussions with a spouse or partner. Do not be surprised if you find these people initially recoiling as they recognize that you are focusing on facilitating their responses. It's like having a good volley in tennis and keeping the ball in the respondent's court. People will perceive your desire to hear what they have to say and to understand their ideas. Their openness to respond will increase.

SESSION 8
Handout 1

Collaborative Meeting Flow Steps: Finding Facts

1. Introduction - The purpose and tone of the meeting are established. Participants are assured that this is a non-blaming, non-punishment meeting and that the goal of the meeting is to develop a plan with which everyone agrees.

↓

2. Finding Facts - This stage identifies the key issues as participants see them. Each person is asked to state his/her one or two chief concerns. The Facilitator starts with the school staff, asking the principal and then the teacher and support personnel to share their chief concerns. Then the Facilitator questions the family about their concerns. Paying attention to the family hierarchy, he/she questions the parents first, and then the siblings and the child with the identified problem.

↓

3. Blocking Blame - While finding facts, the leader blocks blame thereby creating a non-blaming atmosphere. The purpose of the meeting is not to establish blame or decide who or what 'caused' the problem but to use the shared energy of the group to solve the problem.

↓

4. Checking for Consensus - Participants identify the primary topics and/or themes that emerge from finding facts and agree on issues to work on. The leader ascertains that people have a common sense of the definition of the problem.

↓

5. Determining a Decision - The group decides on what issues will be addressed in this meeting. It is made clear which issues they will not make decisions about in this meeting. They determine what if anything should be done to develop a plan to solve the problem. This decision becomes the standard of measure against which to evaluate progress or change.

↓

6. Arriving at Action - The group develops a final plan. The child, the parents, school staff and significant others jointly agree on what specific actions they will take including who will do what, how, when, and where. Group determines a plan for follow-up.

SESSION 8
Handout 2

Finding Facts

Issues

- The facts are the "actions, thoughts and feelings of the participants." They are the basis on which consensus is reached and a solution to the problem developed.
- The step of finding facts consists of each person reporting his or her concerns about the student or the situation.
- The teacher's report serves as a model for others and follows the criteria of:
    1. Set priorities - select the two or three most important things to focus on.
    2. Describe actions.
    3. Give context of observed actions.
    4. Use language the child and family understand.
    5. Be direct – don't pull punches.

Examples

1. Set priorities and be direct:
"There are two things that I'm most concerned about. The first is John's pattern of lateness to school. The second is a change I've observed in how John responds to school."

2. Describe actions and use language the family understands:
"For the last three weeks, John has been late to school nine times. [Have the attendance book there.] I've noticed what looks to me like a very sad expression on his face most of the time. He walks very heavily and his posture is slumped."

3. Give context of observed actions:
"This is different from the way John was in school before. He's never had a lateness problem and he used to respond to school with what looked to me like a lot of energy and enthusiasm."

SESSION 8
Handout 3

Micro Interviewing Skills

10 Words or Less for Questions - When people are highly activated, their ability to use cues decreases. Questions should be short to help respondents be clear about the focus of the question.

Avoid "Yes or No" Questions - A series of yes/no questions establishes the context of an interrogation. Ask a yes/no question only if that is all that you want to know.

Avoid "Why" Questions - Why questions can also establish an interrogative tone. There are usually many possible answers to any why question. Think of how annoying a continual string of why questions from a young child can be. Furthermore, if the respondent finds that the questioner is not satisfied with his/her answer to a why question, it may seem as if the questioner has a "right" answer in mind.

Avoid Double-Barreled Questions - Ask one questions at a time, not two or three.

Put the Verb First -Starting your question or probe with an action verb clarifies to the respondents what an appropriate answer would be. For example, "Describe what happened to …," "Give me an example of what makes you angry," "Tell me more about that…"

SESSION 8
Handout 4

Macro Interviewing Skills

The macro tool kit helps you to select meaningful interventions to get the specific information that you need. It provides a number of different types of interventions that can be used for different purposes.

- When you start investigating an issue and explore something in greater depth, you use **probing.**
    Example: Johnny, you said you'd like to organize a density booth for the science fair. Can you tell us more about how that would work?

- When you want to follow how something works, you use **tracking.**
    Example: Let's see. Mr. B thinks this happens when there are tests. I'm wondering how that unfolds in your class, Ms. R.

- To make an abstract idea more concrete, you use **illustrating**.
    Example: Mrs. G, you remarked that your daughter, Sally, feels she doesn't get help with her project even when she asks. Could you give me an example of what happens when you ask for help, Sally?

- To help someone who has relevant information open up, you encourage that person through **supporting.**
    Example: Joey, I know it's hard to talk with so many adults in the room, but we really want to hear from you so we can figure out how to help you. Would it feel better to whisper to your mom and have her tell the group what you said?

- To speed up or slow down the flow of information, be aware of the **pacing**.
    Example: I'm mindful of the time and want to be sure we come out with a good plan. So I'd appreciate if you could keep your comments brief.

- When you want to pull together a large amount of information, try **summarizing**.
    Example: So let's see if I can bring all these threads together so we can get a big picture of what is going well for Alison and what she might be struggling with.

- To keep someone from continuing in an unproductive direction, you use **blocking**.
    Example: I understand your concern about the students' choice of reading material in ELA, but right now we need to stay focused on planning this science fair.

- To help reconstruct a complex sequence of events, you follow the chronology by **retracing**.

> ***Example:*** You've shared a lot of information about the fight in the cafeteria and I understand your concern that only students of color were suspended. It might be helpful to reconstruct what happened that day so we can determine whether there were unfair disciplinary procedures.

- When you want to provide a different meaning or perspective to information, you present the information in a new light by **reframing**.
    > ***Example:*** I wonder if Michael's ability to disrupt the entire class suggests that he could be a strong, positive leader if we can help him redirect his energy.

SESSION 8
Handout 5

Case Example: Brianna

Brianna, a first grader, is a shy and withdrawn child who does not have any known friends at school. She returned home from school one day very upset and without her lunch box. She told her mother that some of the children had "bullied" her and taken her lunch box. Her mother called the school extremely upset and angry and demanded to know why her daughter was being picked on in class. She insisted on coming in the next day for a meeting to discuss these issues.

End of Session 8

III. Blocking Blame

SESSION 9: How do blaming statements undermine collaboration?

Rationale:

The central precondition for a successful collaborative meeting is creating a safe, respectful environment that is free of blame. Blame can be blocked right from the outset of family-school meetings by taking the position that everyone is doing the best they can. In being able to recognize blaming statements, school staff can work more productively with families, children and each other. Blocking blame frees them from a vicious cycle of accusations that prevent positive movement towards planning and/or problem solving. When blaming statements do occur, specific interventions can be used by the Facilitator and participants to block them and to maintain a collaborative planning, decision-making and/or problem solving focus.

Goals

- To recognize blaming statements.
- To find alternative ways to view the perceived shortcomings of teachers, parents and students.

Handouts/Materials

- *The Family-School-Child Blame Diagram*

Introduction

Say: **One of the biggest fears of school personnel anticipating any sort of meeting with parents is the possibility that if anger and/or blame erupt, they will be unable to deal with it. Likewise, parents often fear coming to school to hear themselves or their child criticized.**

Blame may be communicated explicitly and directly ("You are the worst math teacher my son has ever had") or implicitly and indirectly ("How long have you been teaching?"). Its negative effects are powerful regardless of whether a person is blaming himself or another person. Blame may have an impact on the interaction even when the person making a particular statement did not intend to be blaming. That is, the receiver of the message feels blamed and responds defensively to the perceived blaming statement regardless of the sender's intent. Whether blame is directed at self or other, whether it is direct or indirect, it must be blocked to ensure that effective collaborative planning, decision-making and/or problem solving proceed.

Blaming needs to be blocked because it is absolutely undermining of collaborative problem solving. Effective decision-making and problem solving cannot be built on a platform of blame. When one or more persons in an intervention feel that they are being blamed, they typically stop attending to the topic or problem being discussed and focus on their own reactions to being blamed. They may withdraw, respond with anger, or take the discussion on a tangent.

Today, in the first of two sessions on blocking blame, we will examine how blame occurs. Next time, we will explore techniques for blocking blame, which can make a critical difference in the success of a meeting.

Activity I. Small Group Activity

INSTRUCTIONS

1. Distribute *Family-School-Child Blame Diagram* Handout #1.

2. Ask participants to think of examples of blaming statements typically directed at each member of the system (parents/family, child and school staff including self-blaming statements).

3. Instruct the participants to break into small groups. Participants should share examples of blaming statements (including self-blame) directed at parents/family, student, staff.
Ask participants to use the family-school-child blame diagram to record the statements and to indicate the direction of the blaming statements with arrows in the appropriate direction from the blamer. For example, they may have an arrow from school to family with the following phrases on it: "You need to monitor your child's homework more" or "This child is not getting the attention she should at home."

4. Reporting Out: Say: **What observations or conclusions would you make about how parents/family, the student and school staff blame each other and themselves?**

Observations might include:

> - When a child has a school problem, the parents often blame themselves, the school or society.
> - The teachers or other school staff, in turn, blames themselves, the child, the parents or the administration.
> - The child often blames himself/herself or might blame his/her parents, teachers or friends.

Activity II. Lecturette

INSTRUCTIONS

1. Say: **Collaborative work can only happen when participants take a non-blaming approach. Let's discuss some factors that may contribute to increased understanding of this approach. We will begin with the premise that teachers, children and parents are doing the best they can at this moment. They may be able to do better if the circumstances, meanings, or abilities change.**

- *Teachers may already be overworked, or trying to teach children who have multiple problems in classrooms that are overcrowded.* They may not always be clear about what to do to handle a particular problem. They are doing the best they can under the circumstances. We are not blaming them for the circumstances or the present problem. By collaborating we will arrive at a good solution for everyone concerned.
- *Parents may be pressured by life circumstances, such as poverty, illness, work and parenting demands.* They may be overwhelmed or lack parenting skills. They may not feel supported by the school or feel intimidated about coming to the school. They try to raise their children the best they can. We aim to help their children by working together with them.
- *Students may be scared to admit that they don't know what they're supposed to know or are preoccupied with a crisis at home.* They may have low self-esteem and be afraid to attempt to complete their schoolwork. They may not have the money to buy the kind of clothes they would feel comfortable in, or supplies for school projects. Yet, we must assume that they are doing the best they can under these circumstances. We will collaborate together to change these circumstances, so that the student's achievement will improve.

The purpose of blaming is to accuse and "nail" someone, not to solve problems. We often believe that if we have ascribed blame, we do not have to address the problem ourselves. Therefore, the goal of collaborative work is to increase skills so that each member of the system can move beyond "doing the best they can" to "working together to do even better." Dealing with blame is a critical skill for establishing a context of partnership and collaboration.

SESSION 9
Handout 1

Family-School-Child Blame Diagram

Use this handout to share examples of blaming statements directed at each member of the system by each member of the system, including family, child and school self-blame. Indicate with arrows who is blaming whom and write examples of blaming statements over the arrows you've drawn.

Child

Family   **School**

End of Session 9

SESSION 10: What techniques can help to block blame?

Rationale:

Techniques for blocking blame are simple but extremely powerful tools for dealing with blame when it arises. As individuals become comfortable with these techniques, they feel empowered to cope effectively with a range of emotions while maintaining a positive and constructive outlook. These techniques, like the ones we learned earlier about micro-and macro- interviewing questions for finding facts, may appear simple. In reality, however, they require much practice to master.

Goals

- To expand collaborative skills to include techniques for blocking blame.
- To apply techniques for blocking blame in a variety of role-playing situations.

Handouts/Materials

- *Collaborative Meeting Flow Steps: Blocking Blame*
- *Techniques for Blocking Blame*
- *Examples of Blaming Statements*

Introduction

Say: **In the last session we learned to recognize and understand negative influence blaming statements. Today we are going to identify and learn specific techniques for blocking blame.**

Activity I. Applying Techniques for Blocking Blame

INSTRUCTIONS

1. Say: **I'd like you to think back for a minute to our last session where we identified blaming statements from parent to teacher, teacher to parent, teacher to child, child to teacher, parent to child, teacher to teacher, faculty to administration, etc. Here are some examples of typical blaming statements.**

2. Distribute *Blaming Statements* Handout #3.

3. Say: **Can you think of examples of other blaming statements that have been directed at you?**

   Have participants share out.

4. Say: **Now we can begin to think about how to block these kinds of statements and maintain a collaborative problem-solving focus.**

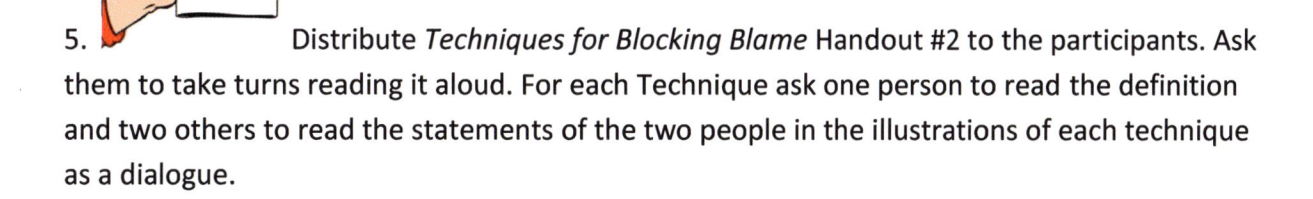

5. Distribute *Techniques for Blocking Blame* Handout #2 to the participants. Ask them to take turns reading it aloud. For each Technique ask one person to read the definition and two others to read the statements of the two people in the illustrations of each technique as a dialogue.

6. Say: **Let's read this out loud to become familiar with each of the techniques. We'll go around the room. For each Technique, I'd like one person to read the definition and two others to read the statements of the two people in the illustrations of each technique as a dialogue. Now let's take one of the blaming statements in the *Blaming Statements* handout and try to apply one of these techniques to it.**

7. After someone has demonstrated the use of one of the techniques ask: **How might one of the other techniques in the handout be used with the same statement?**

8. Have participants try to use several of the techniques on the handout to block a few of the blaming statements on the board.

9. Instruct participants to divide into pairs and decide who is A and who is B. Say: **A's will select one of the statements you would like to learn to block. Tell B which statement you have chosen. Now B's will say this statement to A just as it might be said in the family-school context. A's do your best to block the blaming message and to refocus on the problem and its resolution. Try to make your blocking statements no more than 1 or 2 sentences.**

   After you have completed this, switch roles and do the same sequence again (this time B selects a blaming statement and gives it to A to say to B. B will block the blaming statement).

10. After the participants complete both cycles, call stop.

11. Reporting Out: Ask participants to share examples of blocking blame used in the dyads. Elicit difficulties and address how blame might have been blocked in these examples.

Activity II. Self-Blame

INSTRUCTIONS

1. Say: **It's clear that blaming others is not a productive problem-solving strategy. But neither is blaming oneself. This is true no matter who blames themselves: teachers, students, parents or administrators. Self-blame compartmentalizes the problem and obscures its systemic aspects. It also focuses away from problem solving.**

Often when parents blame themselves it is a way of putting up a barrier. In effect the parent is saying, "I know I have a problem and I'll take care of it. Stay out." Often they propose a solution, and it is tempting to accept it without fully exploring the problem. If you accept the parent's solution offered in haste, it can perpetuate the problem. It puts you as the teacher into an authoritarian rather than a collaborative position. Likewise, when children blame themselves, it may place parents and other concerned adults in the role of rescuer or enforcer rather than involving the child as an active participant in formulating and implementing a solution.

2. *Think About It.* Have participants reflect on the following:

- *How might parents blame themselves?*
- *How might children blame themselves?*

3. List examples.

4. Say: **Let's try using the blocking blame techniques with some examples of self-blame. Break into pairs again, please. A is the teacher and B is the parent. Using the examples we've listed and techniques on your handout practice recognizing and blocking self-blame. Then switch roles.**

5. After 3-5 minutes, instruct the participants: **Now try this again for child self-blame with A as the teacher and B as the child. Block examples of the child's self-blame with techniques on your handout.**

6. Ask participants to share examples of techniques that seemed most effective in blocking the self-blame of the parent and child.

Activity III. Achilles' Heel of Blame

INSTRUCTIONS

1. Say: **Each of us has a particularly vulnerable area which, if targeted for blame by a child, parent, or colleague, would be especially painful or aggravating. One might call this your *Achilles' Heel of Blame.* To identify your Achilles' Heel of Blame, it might be helpful to think about what you pride yourself on most or what you feel most sensitive or vulnerable about. These would be areas where you might have the most trouble blocking blame and maintaining a problem-solving focus. If you become aware of this, you may be able to mobilize more effective strategies for blocking blame. You will also find yourself becoming more confident in your ability to handle even the most challenging interactions with the same professional and collaborative stance.**

2. Say: **Take a moment and think of this area for you. What is your Achilles' Heel of Blame? Share it with your partner.**

Once the partners have shared their Achilles' Heels, ask them to take turns blocking each other's blaming statement using the techniques of blocking blame learned.

Activity IV. Summary Comments

INSTRUCTIONS

1. Say: **Managing blame is our *professional responsibility*. When we rid our school environment of blaming, we have removed one of the most undermining and invalidating toxins in interpersonal relations. We will have accomplished an essential precondition for a collaborative school climate. Colleagues, students and parents will learn from our behavior that "blaming" is not how we do business. Staff, parents and students will come to share the expectation that when a problem exists, people will work together to understand and resolve it.**

SESSION 10
Handout 1

Collaborative Meeting Flow Steps: Blocking Blame

1. Introduction - The purpose and tone of the meeting are established. Participants are assured that this is a non-blaming, non-punishment meeting and that the goal of the meeting is to develop a plan with which everyone agrees.

↓

2. Finding Facts - This stage identifies the key issues as participants see them. Each person is asked to state his/her one or two chief concerns. The Facilitator starts with the school staff, asking the principal and then the teacher and support personnel to share their chief concerns. Then the Facilitator questions the family about their concerns. Paying attention to the family hierarchy, he/she questions the parents first, and then the siblings and the child with the identified problem.

↓

3. Blocking Blame - While finding facts, the leader blocks blame, thereby creating a non-blaming atmosphere. The purpose of the meeting is not to establish blame or decide who or what 'caused' the problem but to use the shared energy of the group to solve the problem.

↓

4. Checking for Consensus - Participants identify the primary topics and/or themes that emerge from finding facts and agree on issues to work on. The leader ascertains that people have a common sense of the definition of the problem.

↓

5. Determining a Decision - The group decides on what issues will be addressed in this meeting. It is made clear which issues they will not make decisions about in this meeting. They determine what if anything should be done to develop a plan to solve the problem. This decision becomes the standard of measure against which to evaluate progress or change.

↓

6. Arriving at Action - The group develops a final plan. The child, the parents, school staff and significant others jointly agree on what specific actions they will take including who will do what, how, when, and where. Group determines a plan for follow-up.

SESSION 10
Handout 2

Techniques for Blocking Blame

DIRECT BLOCKING - Signaling that the purpose of the interaction is not to blame, but to solve a problem.

EXAMPLE: **Student:** Johnny always starts the fights—it's not my fault.
Teacher: We're not here to find out who's to blame but to figure out how you and Johnny can get your work done instead of fighting.

REFRAMING - Providing an alternative point of view about a set of facts which give the facts a more positive, productive meaning.

EXAMPLE: **Teacher:** She gets the other girls in trouble by getting them to break the rules.
Principal: It sounds like Adalia has a lot of leadership potential, but we need to help her direct it in more appropriate ways.

PROBING - Eliciting additional information to clarify the context leading to the blaming.

EXAMPLE: **Student:** You always pick on me.
Teacher: I certainly don't intend to pick on you, David. What do you see me doing that makes you think I'm picking on you? Give me some examples.

REFOCUSING - Redirecting the discussion from a non-productive or nonessential area to an area relevant to helping the student.

EXAMPLE: **Parent:** Derrick's father was always getting into trouble at school and he never finished himself.
Teacher: What do you think makes it difficult for Derrick to do well in school?

ILLUSTRATING - Giving concrete examples of areas of concern.

EXAMPLE: **Parent:** She doesn't act that way at home. You just don't know how to deal with her.
Teacher: What I've observed is that Mary acts that way when she is with her friends. They enjoy talking with each other so much that they don't seem to be able to stop when it's time to get down to work.

VALIDATING - Recognizing the validity of another's perceptions or efforts.

EXAMPLE: **Teacher:** You know, Jose takes up so much of my time and attention I don't have much left over to give to any other child in the class.
Parent: I understand that with 30 children in the classroom there are lots of demands on your time and attention.

AGREEING - Confirming someone's perception of a situation.

EXAMPLE: **Teacher:** It really drives me nuts when people come in and think they can just take over the classroom.
Parent: It would drive me nuts too if I thought someone was trying to take over something that I was responsible for.

SESSION 10
Handout 3

Blaming Statements

1. Johnny never acted like this last year with Mrs. Smith.

2. Johnny has too many learning and emotional problems. I've tried to help but I can't. He should be in special education.

3. No one is doing anything about Ann not doing her homework.

4. I tell him to stop fighting in class all the time and he never listens to me.

5. The mother is never at home and I think the children are being neglected.

6. The parents don't ever seem to follow through on what they need to do.

7. I call the parents to come into school, but they never keep their appointments. They just don't care about their children.

End of Session 10

IV. Creating a Plan

SESSION 11: How are plans created at the end of a collaborative problem-solving meeting?

Rationale:

We've practiced Finding Facts and Blocking Blame. This session will explore the final three stages of the meeting flow process. Contemplating how to integrate the many concerns voiced at a meeting with one student's family or at a multiple family meeting often seems daunting at first. Many teachers, guidance counselors and administrators feel that the process will fail unless they have a preconceived plan. The greatest challenge is learning to "trust the process" and to allow the solution to truly emerge from the collaborative interaction of the group.

Goals
- To understand the final stages of the meeting-flow process.
- To role-play endings of individual and multi-family problem-solving meetings.
- To reflect on the challenges of problem solving.

Handouts/Materials
- Observer notes from Session #8
- *Case Example: Brianna*
- *Collaborative Meeting Flow Steps: Final Three Steps*
- *Sample Problem-Solving Meeting Plans*
- *Checking for Consensus, Determining a Decision and Arriving at Action*
- White board/Smart Board or chart paper

Introduction

Say: **Today we are going to gain experience with the last three steps in the collaborative problem solving process. These critical steps build on the positive non-blaming foundations of the introduction, finding facts and blocking blame stages to come up with a concrete, specific plan. Just feeling better after sharing concerns does not solve a problem. It lays the groundwork upon which a solution is built.**

Activity I. Review of Final Three Steps

INSTRUCTIONS

1. Say: **Let's review these three stages.**

2. Distribute *Collaborative Meeting Flow Steps: Final Three Steps* Handout #2 and *Checking for Consensus, Determining a Decision and Arriving at Action* Handout #4.

3. Ask the group to read the last three stages. Say: **As you review the last three stages:**

   - *What questions come to mind?*
   - *What seems to be the most challenging aspect of actually doing these steps?*

4. Have the group share their responses. List them on chart paper. Identify themes that emerge.

5. Typical issues and some responses to them:

> **ISSUE:** *How do I identify themes?*
> **ANSWER:** We will deal with this process at length in a later session. The answer for now is to look for areas of shared/overlapping concern. Within these areas, identify those issues, which, if worked on are likely to yield the most movement and agreement. A thematic focus is one that organizes a number of topics around one more general idea (i.e. many different examples of a student's getting into trouble may point to a more important general theme that he/she has developed a very bad reputation as a "trouble maker" in the school.)
>
> **ISSUE:** *What if the group does not agree on an issue to work on?*
> **ANSWER:** If this occurs, it may be that the issues which are being identified for them are too specific and that they are not framed in a way which feels inclusive of everyone's concerns. Try to find broader, more overarching themes such as the developmental struggles students deal with e.g., autonomy, making friends, risking success or failure, learning to do things we don't want to do.

ISSUE: *What if the group has no ideas for a plan?*

ANSWER: People new and not so new to these collaborative meeting flow steps often feel at first that they must have a plan ready themselves in case the group can't produce one. Imagining hypothetical plans may help you to feel confident about running the meeting. However, there is a real danger that formulating a plan before going through the process with the group will undermine the collaborative process. The key here is for the plan to emerge from ALL of the participants at the meeting. If people feel heard and not blamed, they are usually very willing to contribute ideas and take responsibility for a plan. Effective use of probing, focusing and summarizing by the group Facilitator will move the group to produce a plan together. Sometimes the leader may use elements mentioned by participants to formulate a proposal for the group to consider as a plan. Such a proposal gives the participants a preliminary plan to react to and they will refine it together to make it fit their own needs. If no one offers suggestions for a plan, it is sometimes helpful to get things moving by presenting a proposal for people to react to.

Activity II. Characteristics of Problem-Solving Meetings

INSTRUCTIONS

1. Say: **It might be helpful to review a few plans from actual meetings with individual families and groups of families.**

2. Distribute *Sample Problem-Solving Meeting Plans* Handout #3.

3. Ask participants to read the plans and to identify characteristics they share.

4. List the characteristics on writing board or chart paper and review them to identify critical ingredients including:

- A clear focus for collaboration on a specific problem.
- A role for everyone at the meeting in the plan.
- Specific, concrete language about who does what, with whom, how often, when and where.
- A set time to follow-up on the plan and determine if it has succeeded.

5. Ask participants how they would improve any of the plans or if they have questions about them.

Activity III. Role-Play

INSTRUCTIONS

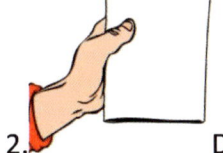

1. Say: **You will now have the opportunity to role-play these three steps. Let's go back to the role-play with Brianna, the shy 1st grade girl.**

2. Distribute *Brianna: Case Description* Handout #1 and notes from that role-play in Session #8.

3. Say: **Please return to the groups you were in when you did this role-play. The notes you received were taken when you conducted the finding facts portion of this meeting. Please get into groups of three. Read these over and, after deciding who will be Brianna, her mother and the teacher, try to:**
   - **CHECK FOR CONSENSUS:** What is the theme you think people can agree on in this situation?
   - **DETERMINE A DECISION:** What does the group decide to work on? What are the first stages of the plan they will develop?
   - **ARRIVING AT ACTION:** What is the specific plan the group decides on? What are the plans for follow-up?

4. *Think About It.* After the groups have worked on this for 10 minutes (maximum) reconvene the participants. Ask them to reflect on the following:
   - *What was the experience like?*
   - *In what ways did it feel successful and/or frustrating?*
   - *Any idea why?*

5. Have the groups share the themes and plans they developed. Compare differences and similarities across groups. Discuss aspects of specific plans that seem especially difficult to accomplish and those that seem geared to the reality of the school environment. Be sure to

point out to participants that no one plan is the *right* plan. Instead, the plan needs to reflect the needs and composition of the group.

6. Say: **Remember, our stance at follow-up meetings toward a plan that was not fully successful, or which was not enacted at all, is that it was a bad plan. If it were a good plan it would have addressed necessary contingencies (e.g., did the teacher have adequate time to do what she had planned?). Our primary aim is to enable the group to continue to collaborate to resolve problems. This collaboration takes place in the course of school life -- not in a series of continuous group meetings.**

SESSION 11

Handout 1

Case Example: Brianna

Brianna, a first grader, is a shy and withdrawn child who does not have any known friends at school. She returned home from school one day very upset and without her lunch box. She told her mother that some of the children had "bullied" her and taken her lunch box. Her mother called the school extremely upset and angry and demanded to know why her daughter was being picked on in class. She insisted on coming in the next day for a meeting to discuss these issues.

SESSION 11
Handout 2

Collaborative Meeting Flow Steps: Final Three Steps

1. **Introduction** - The purpose and tone of the meeting are established. Participants are assured that this is a non-blaming, non-punishment meeting and that the goal of the meeting is to develop a plan with which everyone agrees.

↓

2. **Finding Facts** - This stage identifies the key issues as participants see them. Each person is asked to state his/her one or two chief concerns. The Facilitator starts with the school staff, asking the principal and then the teacher and support personnel to share their chief concerns. Then the Facilitator questions the family about their concerns. Paying attention to the family hierarchy, he/she questions the parents first, and then the siblings and the child with the identified problem.

↓

3. **Blocking Blame** - While finding facts, the leader blocks blame thereby creating a non-blaming atmosphere. The purpose of the meeting is not to establish blame or decide who or what 'caused' the problem but to use the shared energy of the group to solve the problem.

↓

4. ==**Checking for Consensus**== - Participants identify the primary topics and/or themes that emerge from finding facts and agree on issues to work on. The leader ascertains that people have a common sense of the definition of the problem.

↓

5. ==**Determining a Decision**== - The group decides on what issues will be addressed in this meeting. It is made clear which issues they will not make decisions about in this meeting. They determine what if anything should be done to develop a plan to solve the problem. This decision becomes the standard of measure against which to evaluate progress or change.

↓

6. ==**Arriving at Action**== - The group develops a final plan. The child, the parents, school staff and significant others jointly agree on what specific actions they will take including who will do what, how, when, and where. Group determines a plan for follow-up.

SESSION 11
Handout 3

Sample Problem-Solving Meeting Plans

PLAN 1

Background

A family-school meeting was convened for David, a first grader at an inner city school, whose mother and teacher were concerned about his "hyperactivity" and aggressive behavior at school and at home. Present at the meeting were: David's teacher, his mother, David, the school nurse, a teaching assistant and the Facilitator. The group decided that David was an 'expert' at not listening to adults and challenged him to become a new kind of expert --'a listening expert.'

The Plan

1. The nurse and David's mother will follow-up on a previous referral for psychological testing to a local mental health clinic.

2. David will talk with the teaching assistant about what it means to be a 'listening expert' and play listening games with her.

3. When David doesn't listen, the teacher will remind David about being a listening expert by pulling on her ear. Once his listening improves, he will get an 'expert listener badge.'

4. David will talk with his mother each day about how much of a listening expert he was in school.

5. The Facilitator will talk with David's ESL teacher who works with him every day about helping him become a listening expert.

6. A follow-up meeting will be held in a week.

PLAN 2

Background

Akeem is a bright, helpful, friendly third grader in an inner city school. The school was worried about him because he sometimes refused to do what teachers asked him to do especially in large group situations. A family-school meeting was convened to address their concerns about Akeem's behavior. Present at the meeting were Akeem, his teachers, his parents, the principal and acting principal, the special education guidance counselor and the Facilitator. The group decided that Akeem knows the difference between right and wrong. They agreed that they needed to help Akeem understand how his refusal to follow directions creates situations which are not safe for him or others around him. The teacher noted that she enjoys the Akeem who follows directions and does his work and indicated that she would like to help him learn to follow directions.

The Plan

1. When Akeem forgets the importance of following teacher's direction, the teacher will use the secret code they agreed on:

    "Remember what we spoke about...."

2. Akeem will then stop what he is doing and follow directions. He will get a chance to discuss his side with the teacher at a later time.

3. A note will be sent home letting Akeem's parents know that he was successful in keeping the agreement and controlling himself.

4. His parents will reward Akeem with a little something special for his success.

5. A follow-up meeting will be held in two weeks.

PLAN 3

Background

A family-school meeting was convened for Pedro, an inner city second grader who is reluctant to come to school and seems to have serious learning problems. Present at the meeting were his teacher, his mother, Pedro, his two pre-school age sisters, a learning assistant and the Facilitator. The group learned that Pedro's feeling that he was dumb and his fear that other children would tease him about his academic difficulties were contributing to his reluctance to come to the school. They also learned that he likes his teacher and is interested in pleasing her.

The Plan

1. The teacher will refer him for testing to clarify the reasons for his difficulty completing his work and paying attention.

2. The teacher will help Pedro develop an art project with another boy in his class, and will set up a time for Pedro to talk to her about his day.

3. Pedro will mark off every day he comes to school on a chart. He will receive a treat if he comes to school five days in a row.

4. A learning assistant will work with Pedro in the classroom and be his 'special friend.'

5. Pedro's mother will meet with the teacher to identify ways she can help Pedro at home.

6. A follow-up meeting will be held in two weeks.

SESSION 11

Handout 4

Checking for Consensus, Determining a Decision and Arriving at Action

Checking for Consensus
Primary guideline - Identify what will have the most impact for shifting the relationships in the group. This is done by selecting a theme that:
- Allows people to be seen in a different light that will lead to a positive change.
- Provides the group with hope rather than with a renewed adversarial relationship.
- Is a less toxic way of talking about the issue.
- Opens up more options for intervention.

Determining a Decision
- The child should always have an action to do in the plan
- The focus of the plan should be on school-related issues.
- The plan should in some way include the student, teacher, and parents.
- The plan should be appropriate for the roles and positions of the participants.
- The plan should be appropriate for the skill level of the participants.

Arriving at Action
- Who- Who will do the task?
- What- What will the tasks be?
- When- By when will the tasks be done?
- How- What is the standard of quality for doing the tasks?
- Follow-up- How will the plan be evaluated?

End of Session 11

SECTION 4

THE CORE ACTIVITIES: CLIMATE-BUILDING

I. Orientation

SESSION 12: Why is a family-school orientation important?

Rationale:

Although many schools conduct Meet the Teacher or Orientations Nights early in the school year, these events are traditionally structured as an opportunity for one way communication, i.e., for the teachers to talk to the families about expectations and curriculum and to answer parents' questions. Students are not included and the teacher learns little if anything about parents' expectations and students' concerns.

Orientations can be restructured to become important relationship-forming occasions. They can be significant opportunities to send clear messages about how the school wants to work with families in support of children's learning and how family-school collaboration fits into the on-going academic program. Families, children and teachers can engage in three-way conversations about expectations and learning. Parents can participate actively in their child's classroom activities. Teachers and families can get to know each other and develop positive connections, which become the foundation for solving problems that arise and enhancing the learning environment. These bonds will become a resource for the teacher and each family as well as a basis for a community of support for the classroom.

Goals

- To compare traditional and collaborative family-school orientations.
- To review and apply the concepts of climate to activity planning.
- To generate messages that shape the orientation by respectfully conveying the school's commitment to collaboration.

Handouts/Materials

- *Activity Planning Form*
- *Planning for Classroom Family Orientations*
- *Multiple Perspectives Form*
- School calendar
- Chart paper and markers

Introduction

Say: **Today we will focus on building a collaborative climate as early in the school year as possible. This entails utilizing the event, which at most schools marks the opening both of the school year and of the teacher's relationship with the family -- classroom orientation. We will begin by planning classroom orientations for families and children.**

Activity I. New Possibilities for Orientation

INSTRUCTIONS

1. Say: **Let's think for a minute about traditional orientations. The image that a lot of people have is of parents who come to the classroom and sit in the children's desks. What typically happens next?**

2. The group then lists out the elements of a traditional orientation. Possible elements that could be listed include the following:

> - The teacher is at the front of the room.
> - The teacher explains the curriculum for the year and talks about homework policy, how trip permission and money needs to be handled, and the expectations he or she might have for the children.
> - The teacher asks the parents if they have questions and one or two might be asked.
> - The parents go home and may or may not tell their child about what they learned.

3. Say:

- *What kind of relationship is established in this type of orientation?*

- *Who is the expert?*

- *Who sets the tone and identifies the child's needs and goals for the year?*

- *Who gets to know whom?*

4. *Think About It.* Give participants a chance to reflect on and answer these questions:

- *What else could be accomplished through this event?*

- *What would happen if it were 'opened' up to include the child and became a three-way interaction between the teacher, the child and the family?*

5. Explain: **We can see an orientation as a special opportunity for opening communication between families and schools. It is a time to signal to the parents that you at the school are interested in creating a new relationship with them. The orientation can be the first step in establishing a collaborative climate for family-school relations and conveying the message: in this school the way we do business is to be partners with parents. We need your help to ensure your child's success in school.**

We want to change the format of the orientation so that it becomes an activity that begins to restructure the relationship between families and schools. What kind of orientation activity would you create to send this explicit message to students and families: "We want to collaborate with you as partners to ensure your child's success"? One way to think about what you should emphasize in the activity is to consider what you would most want each parent and child to be saying to each other on their way home from the orientation activity.

6. *Think About It.* Ask participants to reflect and report out on the following:

- *What would you want them to say about you and the class program?*

- *What things would you want to do in the activity that would ensure this response?*

7. In the discussion that follows, be sure to highlight and summarize the following points about three critical elements to be included in the activity:

- **FIRST, we want to include the children.** In this way, families and children hear the same things. Seeing his or her parents with the teacher creates a powerful image for the child -- home and school are connected. Seeing the child and parents together provides the teacher with insights into the child's behavior.

- **SECOND, instead of the teacher providing most of the information** in a primarily one-way communication process, the activity will be structured so that the family and child interact with each other and then connect to the teacher. The teacher facilitates, rather than directs, the event.

- **THIRD, we want to prepare children to be at the event** and follow up with them afterwards so that the orientation becomes embedded into their school experience. Their experience in planning, decision-making and/or problem-solving with the central adults in their lives (teachers and parents) becomes part of the overall learning

Activity II. Review of Climate

INSTRUCTIONS

1. **Say: In a previous session, we talked about climate. Let's briefly review the concept of climate so we can think about how family-school orientations can build the kind of climate we most want to achieve in our schools.**

2. Briefly review the concept of climate and its key components with participants. Climate can be broadly defined as having four components (Tagiuri, 1968). These four key areas can be posted on chart paper at the front of the room.

> - **Culture** – The message (beliefs, values, norms).
> - **Milieu** – People and groups (involved together in the environment).
> - **Social Systems** – Patterns of social interactions among participants (what and how they do things together).
> - **Ecology** – Physical characteristics of the environment

CULTURE
As an aspect of climate, culture represents the values, norms and beliefs that are relatively widely shared within the group and which are communicated among the people. One message that might be sent is that education is a shared family-school process. This message can be conveyed through particular curriculum units, like family trees, family stories, and cultural heritage. Another shared value that might permeate the climate is: "We work hard to achieve success."

MILIEU
The milieu refers to the people and groups in the school. A key question regarding the school climate is: How can the similarities and differences among the individuals and groups in the school be viewed as resources for the school? The groups can work together to create a collaborative atmosphere in the school. These groups can be comprised of the school staff, children and families. The groups can be the family-school team, and/or diverse ethnic/racial/cultural groups.

SOCIAL SYSTEM
The social system represents the ways that people interact together in the school. It is that part of the climate that includes what people are doing, their relationships to one another and how they communicate, share and build connections among themselves.

ECOLOGY
The ecology or physical characteristics are those material things that convey a message about people in this environment. They might include welcoming signs to school visitors, displays of children's artwork in the hallways, family bulletin boards, newsletters and letters from the school to the students' families.

In essence, climate is a complex phenomenon integrating the messages sent by everything that goes on in a school: The mission or culture of the school, the characteristics of the members who make up the school, how the school feels to a visitor, a parent, a child or staff member, how the environment is organized, and the relationships as patterns of interaction among these various groups, which may range from whole school meetings to one-on-one teaching.

3. Say: **The form I'm about to pass out stimulates our thinking about climate. We use it as a guide to plan an orientation that builds up a collaborative climate. The form asks us to consider each aspect of climate as we plan a specific activity.**

4. Distribute *Activity Planning Form* Handout #1.

5. Say: **Let's first look at the issue component. What is the issue, or concern, that we want to address in the orientations? As you consider issues for an orientation, think about what 1 or 2 things you would want families and children to discuss with each other that would set the tone of collaboration for the year. What issues would most help you establish a collaborative climate?**

Possible answers include:

- Getting to know the families and children
- Helping the parents and children get to know us
- Building a relationship with the families
- Helping parents feel comfortable in the school
- Showing families that we care about their children
- Finding ways to work together during the school year
- Establishing high standards and expectations for achievement

Activity III. Brainstorming Messages

INSTRUCTIONS

1. Say: **Now, for the activity component: For this situation we have already decided to plan an orientation. For a different situation, we would want to think about the kind of activity that might be used to address other concerns or issues. For example, if we were concerned about children engaging in learning activities during the summer, we might have a "Summer Learning Fair" during the spring.**

    Next, we consider the possible messages that we want to convey. Let's list all the ones we might want to convey in an orientation and then pick a few. Remember, we want to send a message of invitation and interest. As we think about climate, bear in mind that our initial message will set the tone for the year, and signal what kind of climate we are establishing.

2. Record possible messages on the chartpaper.

3. Distribute *Multiple Perspectives Form* Handout #3.

4. Say: **Here is a form that will help us look at the messages. We want to convey messages that are inviting and non-blaming; that focus on working together and hearing from families and children; that build a collaborative climate.**

5. *Think About It.* As you point to the messages on the chart, ask participants to reflect on the following:

    - *How do these messages sound from the perspective of the families? What changes would you want to make?*

- *How do these messages sound from the perspective of the children? What changes would you want to make?*
- *How do these messages sound from the perspective of the teachers and other school staff? What changes would you want to make?*

6. Revise the messages to be as collaborative as possible. Be on the lookout for implicit blame or a lack of respect. For example:

- **The Message:** "We want to help you help your children," conveys the idea that parents need help and are, therefore, deficient in some way. This could be revised to: "We want to work together so children can succeed."

- **The Message:** "We want you to know the services that are provided by the school" also sends the message that parents need services. This could be revised to: "There are many opportunities and supports for children to succeed in this school." This would help the school to think about ways to give information about all of the programs and services the school provides not only to help children who are having difficulty but also to build on their strengths.

7. Say: **Now let's decide on the set of messages that we want to send in our orientations. Which ones should we keep?**

8. List the final messages on new chart paper and keep for the next session.

9. Say: **Finally, before we go on, we should decide on the date for the orientations.**

Issues that need to be considered in deciding the date are:
- Whether each grade will do their orientations on the same day or a different sub-grouping should be used.
- Scheduling them as early as possible, but allowing teachers enough time to do the planning and establish some routines with their children.
- Other activities in the school or community (e.g., Election Day) with which it could conflict.

Give participants 5 – 10 minutes to pencil in a date for orientation on their school calendar, or supply a blank if necessary.

10. Say: **Next time we will continue planning our orientations. We will think about the specific activities that teachers could do with the families. We will also talk about the concerns you might have about including children and think about ways to address these concerns. To prepare for this, take Handout #2 called** *Planning for Classroom Family Orientations* **with you and read it before next time.**

SESSION 12
Handout 1

Activity Planning Form

INSTRUCTIONS: Use the following elements of school climate as a checklist to plan an activity to fulfill a significant educational goal or deal with a major issue of concern at your school.

Issue or Concern: _____

Activity: _____

ELEMENTS OF CLIMATE:

Messages to be conveyed (values, norms, beliefs):

_____
_____
_____
_____

Individual and/or groups who should be involved:

_____
_____
_____
_____

Collaborative interactions necessary to reach goal and convey message:

_____
_____
_____

Physical characteristics of the environment and materials that convey message:

_____
_____

SESSION 12
Handout 2

Planning for Classroom-Family Orientations

PURPOSE OF THE MEETING

For parents, students, and teachers to get to know one another and form a positive partnership to accomplish educational goals.

PARTICIPANTS

Parents and students meet with the teacher in the classroom. It is important for children to be included in the meetings because:

- When children attend the meetings, more parents come.
- The activity provides an opportunity for parents, students, and teacher to talk together about the school year.
- Students can see their parents and teacher talking/working together.
- The activity models how education can be appreciated as a team effort that requires the input of student, parent, and teacher.
- Teachers can see the parents and students interacting and learn more about their students.
- Parents can meet the students with whom their own children are going to school.
- Everyone can hear and respond to the same messages about the school's goals and plans.

TIME/PLACE/INVITATIONS

- Many have found the 9-10 A.M. time best so that parents can come to school with their children, stay for a short time, and then get to work.
- Copy invitations on colorful paper.
- Mention that an official school letter is available for employers.
- Make the meeting open to grandparents, aunts/uncles, or other caretakers if a parent is not available.
- Translate the invitation into other languages if possible.
- In the classroom, children can make additional invitations themselves as a follow-up to the invitation sent by the school.
- Send invitation out two weeks in advance and do a follow-up a few days in advance.

PREPARATION ACTIVITIES

- Prepare students for their role in the meeting. Discuss with them the purpose of the meeting and how they can participate to make it a success. This is an opportunity to help students learn social skills. For example, how do students greet parents at the door, introduce their parents to the rest of the group, and serve refreshments?
- Prepare a class list for circulation at the meeting. Parents can voluntarily write their phone numbers on the sheet. Copies can be distributed to parents for networking, phone chains, etc.

POSSIBLE ACTIVITIES

- Child introduces self and parent.
- Parent and child discuss between themselves one or more of the following and then report out to the rest of the group:

    a. *CHILD:* What is special about me?

    PARENT: What is special about my child?

    b. *CHILD:* When I think of school, I feel _____.

    PARENT: When I think of my child beginning ____ grade, I feel _____.

    c. *CHILD:* What do I especially want to learn this year?

    PARENT: What do I especially want my child to learn this year?

    d. *CHILD/PARENT:* What was the most positive experience I remember about school? What was something that was difficult for me in school?

    e. *PARENTS (especially foreign born):* What was school like in my country?

    A group discussion can follow which will enable the teacher to discuss his/her goals and methods of reaching them. This needs to be done in language the children can understand.

- Elicit special skills or interests that parents have which they could contribute to the classroom.
- Recruit volunteers for other classroom jobs.
- Discuss how parents can best help their children with school. Find out from the parents what their ideas are. Then, work together to set realistic goals. For example, what parents should do with homework is often confusing. Should they: check to make sure it's done? Check to make sure it's done *correctly*? Help them do the homework? Give

them additional work to do? What should parents do if they find their child simply doesn't understand the work?

CONSIDERATIONS

- Parents who speak another language - Can a parent translate for other parents?
- Children without participating parents - The teacher can ask if a parent would act as a "substitute parent" or "special adult" for that child in the day's activity.

SESSION 12
Handout 3

Multiple Perspectives Form

School

_____

_____

_____

_____

_____

_____

Parents

_____

_____

_____

_____

_____

_____

Children

_____

_____

_____

_____

_____

_____

End of Session 12

SESSION 13: What might a specific family-school orientation look like?

Rationale:

A critical element in planning a family-school orientation is designing activities that successfully incorporate parents and children and simultaneously convey an accurate picture of classroom life. As teachers, students, and their families benefit from these orientations, they will realize what a valuable resource they are for establishing a positive and comfortable relationship early in the school year. These ties become the basis for other preventive and celebratory family-school interactions and lay a firm foundation for intervening when problems arise.

Goals

- To identify orientation activities that reflect the specific messages that participants wish to convey.
- To plan for classroom orientations.

Handouts/Materials

- *Activity Planning Form*
- Chart paper with possible "Messages" for the orientation listed (from last session)
- Chart paper and markers

Introduction

Say: **Last session, we penciled in an orientation date and decided on the messages that we wanted our orientations to convey. We will continue today and plan the activities that will make up the orientation program.**

Activity I. Specific Activities

INSTRUCTIONS

1. Distribute *Activity Planning Form* Handout #1.

2. Say: **Some teachers want a lot of flexibility in what they do in their classrooms. Others would like the plan to be much more specific so that they can even divide labor among their colleagues in preparing materials. Let's brainstorm possible ideas for activities so we can then have a better idea of how to execute them.**

In planning the activities for the orientation, we want to make sure they are collaborative and communicate the messages we want to send about the school climate. This means:

- School staff, parents and children are interacting together --parents are not the audience to something the child or the teacher does.
- There is reciprocal communication between families and the teacher as the significant adults in the children's lives.

Let's keep these two criteria and our message in mind as we plan the activities. What activities might be developed for some of the themes we've listed?

3. List possible activities on the board.

4. *Think about it.* Ask participants to reflect on the following:

- *Are these activities interactive in the sense that children and parents are working together?*
- *Do these activities provide a way for families to communicate to the teacher?*

- *Do these activities provide a way for the teacher to communicate to the families?*

- *Do these activities convey the message(s) we want to send to families?*

- *Do these activities build a collaborative climate?*

5. Say: **Do you want to pick one activity and have everyone do the same one or do you want to choose among these ideas and develop it yourself?**

If the group decides to do the same activity, then you might want to divide labor on developing the materials and more specific instructions.

6. Write the final ideas for the activities on chart paper so you can bring it to the next meeting.

7. Explain to participants that in mapping out specific activities that structure interactions in a collaborative way they have addressed the "Collaborative Interactions Necessary" section of the Planning Form.

8. Say: **The final section of the planning form that we will briefly examine today is the physical characteristics section. This section is linked to the ecology of the school climate:**

- *How will the physical environment be used to send the messages you want to convey?*

- *What kinds of things should be displayed in the classroom to convey the message?*

- *How should the room be arranged to convey the message? Should chairs be placed in a circle? For example, should the teacher sit at the same level and in the same type of chair as everyone else?*

- *What materials should be available for families to look through and work with?*

Next time we'll plan the specific logistics of the event, e.g., invitations, getting parents from the door of the school to the classrooms, etc.

SESSION 13
Handout 1

Activity Planning Form

INSTRUCTIONS: Use the following elements of school climate as a checklist to plan an activity to fulfill a significant educational goal or deal with a major issue of concern at your school.

Issue or Concern:
_____

Activity:
_____

ELEMENTS OF CLIMATE:

Messages to be conveyed (values, norms, beliefs):
_____
_____
_____

Individual and/or groups who should be involved:
_____
_____
_____

Collaborative interactions necessary to reach goal and convey message:
_____
_____
_____

Physical characteristics and materials that convey the message:
_____
_____
_____

End of Session 13

SESSION 14: What are the final steps of family-school orientation planning?

Rationale:

In planning an activity successfully, special attention must be paid to preparing the children. Since the children are the focus of family-school collaboration, it is especially important that they be ready to participate actively and understand the purpose of the event for themselves and the adults.

Goals

- To understand specific ways to prepare children for the family-school orientation.
- To identify specific tasks to be completed before, during, and after the orientation.

Handouts/Materials

- *Family-School Planning Checklist*
- *Activity Feedback Form*
- Chart paper with the "messages" for the orientation listed
- Chart paper with the orientation activities listed
- White board/Smart Board or chart paper

Introduction

Say: **Today we will do the nitty-gritty logistical planning that will make our orientations successful. Here is the family-school planning checklist. I can guarantee that if you do everything on this checklist you will have a successful orientation.**

Activity I. Invitations

INSTRUCTIONS

1. *Think about it.* Ask participants to reflect on the following:

- *How do you invite people in a way that signals that this orientation is the first step in creating a collaborative partnership between families and the school?*

2. Give participants an opportunity to respond to this question and then incorporate their thoughts into suggestions for generating the two following types of invitations.

3. Say: **First, let's talk about invitations.**

The school should send out a formal invitation in the form of a flyer, letter, etc. This is helpful because it signals to the parents that this is a school-wide event that has the support of the administration and that all the other classes will be meeting with their families as well. It is essential that the school's invitations convey the messages you have chosen. After the invitations are drafted, it is helpful to read them with the question "What message does this convey to the families?" in mind.

4. Decide who will be in charge of writing the invitation and the date it will be distributed with the children. Pencil this in to the school calendar.

5. Say: **The Children's Invitation:**

The most important invitation, however, is the one that the children create themselves in the classroom. Teachers of younger children may want to give them a partially complete invitation that they will then further color, decorate, or complete. This is one of the ways that children will become more involved and get excited about having their parents come to the classroom. They will be the "ambassadors" to their parents, drawing them into the activity. Engaging students in a discussion of the purpose of the meeting and how that purpose can be communicated in the content of the invitation clarifies expectations for their participation in the meeting. They become invested in the meeting as an activity focused on their own school life. They understand that only they know what they are thinking and feeling about their learning experiences. They have an important role to play in informing the teacher and parents about their school experiences. They can also seek help with specific problems.

Get volunteers to make up the invitation format for the group. Decide when the invitation will be created, copied, distributed among the teachers, and sent out with the children. Ask the children to discuss the importance of the activity with their parents.

Activity II. Family-School Checklist Planning

INSTRUCTIONS

1. Distribute *Family-School Planning Checklist* Handout #1.

2. Say: **Now let's go over each of the items on the Family-School Planning Checklist to see what still remains to be done and when it should be done.**

If participants are not from the same school, they can work on these details with colleagues from their own school in small groups. Or, they can review this section with an eye toward how to apply it to their school.

3. Go through each item on the checklist and decide who will do it and when it will be done. Make sure that either at the next meeting, or in person, the coordinator for the event gets a report on how things are progressing. Points to make on selected items include:

> **"Before the Activity":**
>
> In general, a detailed agenda needs to be planned to make sure that all movement of people through the building is covered. For example, how will the parents come into the building? Do they need to sign in? Are we going to have 150 parents trying to sign in all at once? Can we have several tables open for this? Should the parents meet in the auditorium to be greeted by the principal and others before they go to the classrooms? (If they do this, then all the parents will move into the classroom at the same time and the teacher won't have to worry about parents coming in a few at a time.) If there are refreshments, should they be served in the auditorium or served in the classrooms?
>
> **The agenda might look something like this:** [Write on chart paper]
>
> | | |
> |---|---|
> | **08:40-09:00** | Parents arrive in auditorium, sign in, and have coffee and cake. |
> | **09:00-09:20** | Greetings by the principal, family school coordinator, PTA president. |
> | **09:20-09:30** | Move to classrooms and get seated in classrooms |
> | **09:30-09:40** | Introductions |

09:40-10:10	Activity
10:10-10:30	Discussion
10:30-10:35	Parents fill out feedback form

4. Say: **Many times children are the key to bringing the parents to the activities. Having them create invitations is one way to simultaneously involve them in and inform them about the orientation. Discussing the orientation with them beforehand is also important. They can:**
- **Discuss expectations of themselves and the event.**
- **Plan ways of greeting adults and showing them around the classroom.**
- **Offer suggestions about how to organize activities.**
- **Decide who should play what roles, e.g., set-up, clean-up greeters, guides, etc.**

If children are involved in the planning, this does two things:
- **They get more excited about their parents coming to school. They will know more about what's going on and can convey that to the parents.**
- **They can build their skills of responsibility-taking, group work, planning, and social interaction.**

5. Remind participants: **Some children won't have their parents there. The teacher should discuss this with the children beforehand and let the children know what will happen if their parents are not there. For example, you may want to ask the parents who are there to double up and work with two children. You can assure the children that no one will be left out of the activity.**

6. Additional Issues:

Gauge whether the group needs an additional session to cover anything else. Often teachers need additional help in planning the interactive activity and firming up the logistics so that everyone knows exactly what will occur and when. If this is the case, plan an additional session or two to cover these issues.

Make clear that attending to all details in the planning phase will ensure a successful activity. Moreover, once they have implemented a collaborative family-school orientation the first time, they will be able to use this experience to enhance subsequent orientations. The aim is to build routines for implementing this activity that becomes second nature for the staff, students and families.

SESSION 14
Handout 1

Family-School Planning Checklist

Before the Activity

- ☐ Make sure that the date picked for the activity is not conflicting with other school or district activities.
- ☐ School has sent an official invitation about the Family-School Activity approximately 1 ½ weeks before the activity.
- ☐ Parents are informed that the school will provide official letters to employers asking that parents be excused to attend Family-School Activity.
- ☐ Focusing question forms, if appropriate, have been sent home to help families begin thinking about their participation in the activity.
- ☐ Children have discussed how and why the activity will be conducted and how to behave to make it a success.
- ☐ Children prepare an attractive invitation telling the time, place and nature of the Family-School Activity and send them about 3 days before the workshop for parents to sign. Children return signed invitations to classroom teachers.
- ☐ Activities and materials have been prepared which allow for parent/teacher/child involvement and interaction.
- ☐ If applicable, refreshments have been purchased and a plan for setting up and cleaning up has been developed.
- ☐ A decision is made whether parents will come into a common space, e.g., auditorium, and be greeted there before going as a group up to the classrooms.
- ☐ If parents need to sign into the school for security purposes, provisions have been made to accommodate a large number of parents signing in at once.
- ☐ Nametags are available for parents when they arrive at the classroom.
- ☐ Classroom furniture has been rearranged, if necessary, to accommodate interactive activities.
- ☐ Parent feedback forms have been developed and copied and are ready to distribute to parents.

During the Activity

- ☐ If applicable, directions for participation are clearly spelled out and placed in a visible spot for parents to see as they arrive.
- ☐ Parents are greeted, asked to sign in (if they haven't done so already), and to sit with their child or at an assigned table/area. If they have coats, they put their coats in a place that will not interfere with the activity.

- ☐ Parents are assigned as "table parents" or "parents for a day" for children whose parents do not attend.
- ☐ Explain to children that not all parents could attend because of other obligations but hopefully they will come another time. Everyone present will benefit from today's activity.
- ☐ Explain that parents will be taking an active role in the activity and will be participating with their child and the class.
- ☐ Have parents introduce themselves or have children introduce their parents.
- ☐ Circulate around the classroom to work with family groups during interactive activities. Provide a follow-up activity that parents can do at home with their child.

After the Activity

- ☐ Give parents letters to their employer explaining the importance of the day's activity or remind them to pick them up from the main office.
- ☐ Affirm that this is the beginning of your work with the parents and children as partners to provide the best education for the children.
- ☐ Ask parents to complete the feedback forms before they leave. Collect the forms.
- ☐ Provide light refreshments to help create a pleasant atmosphere (optional).
- ☐ Thank parents for their attendance and acknowledge their interest and concern for their child's education.
- ☐ Send thank you notes home to those parents who participated.
- ☐ Send a brief description of the event to parents who were absent, indicating that they were missed and how they might follow-up on the activity with their child at home. Encourage their participation in upcoming events.
- ☐ Talk with the children about their reactions to the event and their evaluation of the event as a whole. An evaluation form or writing assignment might be a useful experience to kick-off an evaluation discussion.

SESSION 14
Handout 2

Activity Feedback Form

Date of Activity: _____

Name (optional): _____ Child's Classroom: _____

1. What did you like most about today's events?

_____

_____

2. How different was this activity from events that you have attended before at schools? *(Circle one, with 1 being not at all different and 7 being extremely different)*

1   2   3   4   5   6   7

How was it different?

_____

_____

3. How helpful was this in learning about your child's life at school? *(Circle one, with 1 being not at all helpful and 7 being extremely helpful)*

1   2   3   4   5   6   7

Check all the items that were helpful:

_____ I got to know the teacher better.

_____ The teacher got to know me better.

_____ I was able to see my child in the classroom.

_____ I was able to see my child's work in the classroom.

_____ My child was excited that I came to school.

_____ I got to see the other children my child goes to school with.

_____ I was able to meet some of the other parents in the classroom.

_____ I showed my child that I cared about him/her.

_____ I got ideas for helping my child.

_____ Other _____

4. What would you like to see done at future events where students, parents, and teacher meet together?

_____

_____

Other comments:

_____

_____

End of Session 14

II. Family-Teacher Conferences

SESSION 15: How do we transform parent-teacher conferences into family-teacher conferences that include the child?

Rationale:

Collaboration can become business as usual in a school. Its focus is less on what is done between families and school than on *how* it is done. Routine school events like twice-yearly parent-teacher conferences can be transformed into collaborative family-teacher meetings by including the child.

Goals

- To simulate conferences with and without the child present.
- To plan specific ways to prepare children for conferences.
- To role-play conferences following a planning form that includes abridged meeting flow steps.

Handouts/Materials

- *Open-School Conference Planning*
- *Planning To Include The Child*
- *Getting Yourself Ready for Family-Teacher Conferences*
- *Case Example: Sarah Wilson*
- White board/Smart Board or chart paper

Introduction

Say: We have thus far transformed one school-wide event, the orientation, into a family-school activity. In this session we are going to discuss and practice ways to create another core family-school event. We are going to change parent-teacher conferences into family-teacher conferences in which the student is an active participant. We will do this primarily by including the child and following the meeting flow steps. Today, we will focus on getting the "feel" of a conference that includes the child in this way.

Warm-Up

1. *Think about it.* Ask participants to recall their own experiences as children waiting for their parents to return from conferences with their teachers. Have them consider the following:

   - *How did it feel to wait to hear news of your school progress from your parents?*
   - *What were your thoughts about yourself, your parents and your teacher while you waited?*
   - *What were your reactions to the 'news' your parents brought home from the meeting – especially if it was negative or critical?*

   Ask a few volunteers to share their memories with the group.

2. Ask the group to consider now what it would have felt like for them to be included in the conferences. Ask a few individuals to share their thoughts with the group.

3. Record the feedback. Possible responses might include:

   - Scary
   - Confusing
   - Empowering
   - Overwhelming
   - Informative
   - Burdening
   - Revealing
   - Helpful

Activity I: Child Out/Child In Role Play

INSTRUCTIONS

1. **Say: To give you an opportunity to address this issue in depth, we are going to do a role-play, which will allow you to compare a family conference without the child to one with the child present.**

2. Select participants to play the roles of teacher, mother, father and child. Based on the participants' preference and/or school needs, the role of guardian could be swapped to reflect a more realistic scenario.

3. Say: **We are going to role-play a typical teacher conference. Jerry Houston is a third grade student at a suburban elementary school. He is a bright boy who is not doing as well as his teacher Mrs. Rufus thinks he should, especially in math. He is an avid reader, but tends to read books he likes during math lessons. Jerry has two or three close friends with whom he enjoys doing special projects. Otherwise his participation in class is sporadic.**

4. Direct role-players to conduct a conference between Mrs. Rufus and Jerry's parents, Mr. and Mrs. Houston. Stop the role-play after 2-3 minutes.

5. Direct role-players to start the conference over again completely, including Jerry with his parents and teacher in this version of the role-play. Stop the role-play after 3-5 minutes.

6. *Think about it.* Ask the group to reflect on the following, and lead these questions into a discussion:

   - *What differences did you (the non role-players) notice between the two role-plays?*

   - *For the adult role-players, how would you characterize the experience of being in the two conferences? In which one were you most comfortable? Which one was most productive?*

   - *For the child role-player, how did it feel to be in the conference? Did you feel heard? Respected? What did you gain from the experience?*

   - *How, if at all, did the behavior of the adults differ? In which role-play was there the most defensiveness? In which the most collaborative?*

Activity II. Preparing Children

INSTRUCTIONS

1. Remind participants about their reactions to the child-in/child-out role-play.

2. Say: **Merely being present in the meeting does not guarantee that children will have a good experience. What children imagine teachers might say about them is usually worse than the reality of what the teachers will actually say. Children need to be carefully prepared for participation in these meetings so that it can become a meaningful and positive experience for them and the adults.**

3. Distribute *Planning To Include The Child* Handout #2 and *Getting Yourself Ready For Family-Teacher Conferences* Handout #3. Review with participants.

Activity III. Reviewing the Advantages of Family-Teacher vs. Parent-Teacher Meetings

INSTRUCTIONS

1. Distribute *"Open-School Conference Planning"* Handout #1 and lead a discussion listing the advantages of collaborative twice-yearly conferences including:

> - **Children hear** positive feedback in the presence of their parents.
>
> - Children can hear **teacher's feedback directly**, not filtered through their parents.
>
> - **Parents' responses** to the teacher's report can be better directed by the teacher.
>
> - **If students deny a behavior**, (e.g., frequently telling their parents they have no homework) it can be dealt with directly.
>
> - **With all the participants present**, the conference can become a mini-problem-solving session. A specific behavior can be targeted for improvement and an agreement negotiated to resolve it (including specific steps to be taken by parents, teacher and child).
>
> - **Students see parents and teacher in agreement** about class expectations.
>
> - **The teacher learns** more about the student by observing him/her interacting with the parents.
>
> - **Parents experience the teacher** as concerned and supportive.
>
> - **It increases the available resources** for problem-solving since the child's perspective and participation is available to, and solicited by, the parent and teacher.
>
> - **Being included** in the process increases the child's responsibility-taking as well as his/her reflective and problem solving abilities.

Activity IV. The Meeting Itself

INSTRUCTIONS

1. Say: **We will now focus on the conference itself. We will discuss the framework for the meeting and you will have an opportunity to role play a family-teacher conference in small groups. Because we haven't gone over the collaborative meeting flow steps yet, pretend that this is a conference you've had, but now the child is there as well.**

2. Say: **Remember to start with something positive about the child (i.e., his/her strengths). You may also be talking not only about concerns but communicating what you see as the messages, points of emphasis, or important information for this meeting. For example, something you want a student to be challenged by or requests for feedback on ongoing or completed classroom activities.**

3. Break participants into groups of 4 for role-play of Family-Teacher conference. Participants are to assign themselves the following four roles: *Teacher, Mother, Father and Child.* Some groups may want to enact meetings with single parents or other family members or guardians (grandparents, aunts or uncles, foster-care parents). Explain that they will rotate these roles as the role-play progresses.

4. Distribute *Case Example: Sarah Wilson* Handout #4. Participants can either create their own scenario -- deciding on the grade level and gender of the child, the child's strengths and weaknesses, and particular areas they'd like to discuss with the parents and child, or they can use the handout's scenario.

5. *Think about it.* Reassemble the large group and ask them the following focus questions:

- *How would this conference have been different in tone and outcome if Sarah had not been included?*

- *What are the benefits and drawbacks to this format from your perspective?*

- *What was accomplished through the collaborative process -- i.e. Sarah's presence -- which is unusual for a traditional routine Teacher-Parent Conference?*

- *From the perspective of the teacher, how worthwhile was this format compared to a typical Parent-Teacher Conference?*

- *What types of plans did the groups who role-played Sarah Wilson's situation come up with?*

- *What was it like to be Sarah at this conference? What were the benefits of being at the meeting for Sarah?*

- *Now that you've experienced a Family-Teacher Conference, what would you say are key elements to having it run well and productively for everyone?*

SESSION 15
Handout 1

Open-School Conference Planning

OVERVIEW

In the context of restructuring a number of regular school and classroom activities in order to establish a more cooperative relationship between families and the school, schools have restructured parent-teacher conferences into family-teacher conferences by inviting students to be present during these meetings. The advantages to these types of conferences include:

- Children can hear positive feedback in the presence of their parents.
- Children can hear the teacher's feedback directly and not filtered through their parents' perceptions.
- Parents' responses to the teacher's report can be better directed by teachers;
- If students deny a behavior (claiming to be picked on by the teacher), this can be dealt with directly.
- With all participants present, the conferences can act as mini problem-solving sessions. A specific behavior can be targeted for improvement and an agreement negotiated to resolve it (including specific steps to be taken by child, parent and teacher).
- Student sees teacher and parent in agreement about class expectations.
- The teacher learns more about the student by observing him or her in interaction with the parents.
- Parents experience the teacher as concerned and supportive.
- It increases the available resources for problem solving since the child's perspective is available to the parent and teacher, and the child's participation in developing a plan is also solicited.
- Being included in the process increases the child's responsibility-taking.

PLANNING

1. Children need to be formally invited so parents know that they are to bring their child. This can be done through letters sent home with the children or through telephone calls to parents. *Giving children verbal messages to take to their parents is not an effective way to invite them to the meetings.*

2. Children also need to prepare for the meeting. What children imagine teachers might say about them is usually worse than the reality of what the teachers will actually say. Possible ways of preparing children include:
  - Children fill out their own report card and compare them with the teacher's evaluation
  - Children identify strengths and areas in need of improvement

- Teacher and children role-play a conference in class
- Teacher leads discussion with children about what they imagine the conference to be like -- fears or concerns, what they might look forward to. This could be done in whole language format: write in journal, draw a picture.
- Children choose work they would like their parents to see.
- Children write a letter to their parents and have a space for the parent to respond.

In general, preparation should be integrated into the curriculum. This preparation touches upon expression, problem solving, anticipation, planning and taking responsibility for an event, self-reflection, and social skills.

IMPLEMENTATION

1. If the meetings are held in the classroom, make a small area where the teacher, parents, and student can sit in a circle. The lack of physical barriers such as a desk or table will facilitate open communication.

2. While parents and children are waiting, the children could give their parents a tour of the room, showing them where they sit, their folder of work, the artwork on the walls, etc. Most teachers who have done this have not found it to be distracting to the conferences that are taking place in a corner of the classroom away from the traffic pattern. Some schools use an appointment schedule.

3. One way that information could be presented is to start with the child's evaluation of himself or herself. The child could report the one or two things that he/she does well and the one or two things that he/she has trouble with.

4. If there are serious problems that require a more extensive meeting, don't attempt to solve these problems in the family-teacher conference. Instead, use the conference as a time to connect with the family and to set the stage for a problem-solving meeting to be held at a later date.

5. To run the actual meeting, teachers have found it helpful to use the following sequence of steps as a guide:

   a. Finding Facts
      1. Set priorities - before the conference, select the one or two most important things to focus on.
      2. Describe actions or behavior sequences concretely.
      3. Give context of observed actions.
      4. Use language the child and family understand.
      5. Be direct and non-blaming about your concerns.

b. Blocking Blame

1. Present problems in such a way that it focuses attention on the student's education (not on family) and thus establishes a context for problem solving. It does not help to have families feeling blamed.
2. The objective of the meeting is to clarify the situation and find a solution.
3. Block parents' blame by feeding back to them and emphasizing their underlying concern for their child, which you understand and share.
4. Use objective data, not feelings or impressions (e.g., attendance records, quiz results, specific observations.)

c. Checking for Consensus

1. Identify areas of concern about which everybody agrees in order to establish a focus for planning solutions.

d. Determining a Decision

1. Focus on an aspect or perspective of the problem where change can be clearly identifiable, measurable and do-able. Do not try to do too much.
2. The plan should in some way include the student, teacher and parents. For example, the plan may involve the parent and student, but some feedback to the teacher is also included in the plan.
3. Do not ask anyone to do more than they can do -- keep the initial steps small but meaningful.

e. Arriving at Action

1. Write the plan down. Include everybody's commitments -- who will do what, when, where and how.
2. Include a way to follow-up on progress, e.g., a follow-up meeting at an appropriate time, a planned phone call, or exchange of letters.

SESSION 15
Handout 2

Planning To Include the Child

1. **Children need to be formally invited** so that parents know that they are supposed to bring their child. This should be done through letters and/or phone calls to the parents from the teacher. A formal letter from the principal to all parents is important to give the rationale and to legitimize this approach for the whole school or specific grades (especially when this approach is introduced for the first time).

2. **Children also need to prepare for the meeting.** Here are some suggested steps for doing this:

    - ☐ Let the children know that they are going to be included in a conversation with you (teacher) and their families about how things are going in class for them. Explain to the class that when they come to the meeting, you would like them to participate in the discussion with the grown-ups.

    - ☐ Explain to them that you and they are going to take the time to help them get really ready to be an important part of the meeting. Explain that they are first going to think about themselves, and then have a conversation with you. Then, they will imagine what it will be like to have their parents there with them.

    - ☐ Explain that the most important thing they can do to get ready is to begin to think about themselves and how they are doing in class.

    - ☐ Distribute the *Getting Yourself Ready for Family-Teacher Conferences* form to older children and ask them to complete this on their own (these forms should be used as a model to be adjusted for students of different ages). Read questions to younger children and ask them to think about it and remember what they think, or have them dictate their answers to an adult.

    - ☐ Explain to the students that at the conference, you and they will have a conversation with their families about how things are going. Indicate that first you and they will have a conversation together about the handout they just completed. As time permits, have a brief meeting with each child to discuss his/her responses to the handout or role-play such a discussion with a few children in front of the class. Indicate where you agree with their responses and point out additional strengths and areas in need of improvement.

    - ☐ Ask the children what it would be like to include their parents in a meeting like this. Ask the students to share their expectations and feelings about what it will be like to have their parents there.

- ☐ Invite the children to role-play a family-teacher conference with you as the teacher and another adult or a student as the parent. As the class observes, the teacher can start the meeting by asking the student to talk first about his/her strengths and areas needing improvement or new learning. Then demonstrate how the teacher and the parents might respond.

- ☐ Give a few students the opportunity to participate in the role-play. Ask the class for feedback about the experience and discuss how their expectations have changed from the time you first mentioned that they were going to be included in the conferences. Children should think of themselves as the *world expert* on themselves. Only they can know what they are actually thinking or feeling. This is why it is so important for them to be an active participant in the meeting. Help the students to see the meeting as one that they and the teacher are inviting parents to join.

- ☐ Ask the class for suggestions about how to invite their families to the conferences so they will know what to expect. This discussion can lead to the creation of student-made invitations to their families.

SESSION 15
Handout 3

For Students: Getting Yourself Ready for Family-Teacher Conferences

One of the ways to get ready for meeting with your family and the teacher is to begin to think about yourself and all the things you've learned and done in this class so far. Here are some questions to answer that will help you think about how things are going for you in our class.

Please read and answer these questions.

1. **Something I can do now that I couldn't do last year is:**

   _____

   _____

2. **Something I'm trying hard to learn is:**

   _____

   _____

3. **The things I do well in this class are:**

   _____

   _____

4. **Some of the things I would like help with are:**

   _____

   _____

5. **My favorite activity in this class is:**

   _____

   _____

Student's Signature: _____   Date:_____

SESSION 15
Handout 4

For Parents: Family-Teacher Conferences Preparation Form

1. What do you want your child to accomplish for the remainder of the school year?

_____

_____

2. What questions do you have about your child in school that you would like to talk about at this conference?

_____

_____

3. Are there any changes at home that you would like to share with us?
These changes may affect his/her behavior and work in school.

_____

_____

4. Are there any other concerns that you have?

_____

_____

Note: Please bring this form with you to the conference with your child's teacher.

Name of Student: _____   Class _____

Parent/guardian: _____   Date: _____

SESSION 15
Handout 5

Three-Way Conference Summary Form

Issue to work on:

_____
_____
_____

How it will be worked on:

    The Student will:

    _____
    _____
    _____

    The Parent will:

    _____
    _____
    _____

    The Teacher will:

    _____
    _____
    _____

We will follow up on progress by:

Date: _____

Student Signature:_____   Parent Signature:_____

Teacher Signature(s):_____

SESSION 15
Handout 6

Family-Teacher Conference Case Example: Sarah Wilson

Sarah Wilson is a bright, overweight fifth grader who does very well in reading and language arts. She is less proficient and makes careless errors in math. Her behavior in class is appropriate when activities are structured; she is confident in that subject area and clear about expectations for the task. Recently, Sarah has been telling her parents that she is unhappy and has been picking on smaller children and getting into fights with peers. Sarah's mother is very worried about her social adjustment and wants very much to help Sarah develop positive friendships with other girls. Her father is more concerned about seeing her math grades and comprehension improve and would like to see her mother become less fretful about Sarah.

End of Session 15

III. Family-School Problem-Solving Meetings

SESSION 16: What is a family-school problem-solving meeting?

Rationale:

This section of the manual provides step-by-step instruction in conducting productive, collaborative problem-solving meetings with families. Revisiting the meeting flow steps in greater depth, we explain how to convene meetings where blame is blocked and the resources of the family and school are harnessed to enhance children's learning and development.

Goals

- To clarify the purpose of family-school problem-solving meetings.
- To review the meeting flow steps as the basis for problem-solving meetings before going more in depth.
- To practice introductions to family-school problem-solving meetings.

Handouts/Materials

- *Collaborative Meeting Flow Steps: Introduction*
- *Examples of Introductions to Family-School Meetings*
- *Steps to Our Family-School Problem-Solving Meeting*

Introduction

Say: Today we will begin to address the issue which most frequently draws teachers' and school administrators' attention to families: the need to contact parents about a problem their child is experiencing in school.

We will begin to learn how to conduct productive, collaborative problem-solving meetings with individual children and their families. These meetings minimize blame and maximize the ability of the family and school to work together on the child's behalf. As this meeting becomes a routine problem-solving vehicle, children, staff, parents and other family members develop general expectations that they will be able to discuss and resolve problems in ways they all value.

In this session we will briefly review the meeting flow steps that form the backbone of these meetings and focus primarily on positive ways to introduce and set an optimistic tone for the meeting.

Activity I. Reflection

INSTRUCTIONS

1. *Think about it.* Ask participants to reflect privately about their most difficult experiences either as parents, students, or teachers (school personnel) in meetings about a problem in school. Have them consider and reflect on the following:

   - *What was the hardest part of the meeting for you? Why?*
   - *What got in the way of resolving the problem in the meeting?*
   - *What would have had to happen for you to feel that the meeting was a success?*

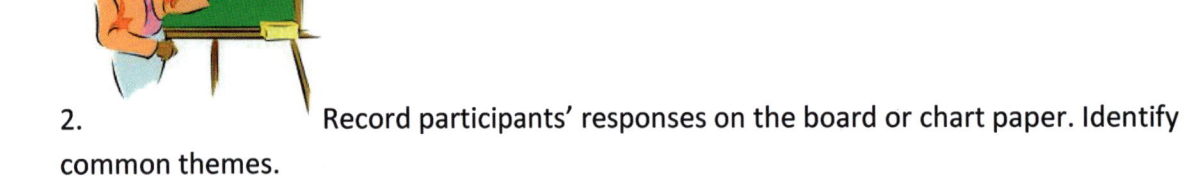

2. Record participants' responses on the board or chart paper. Identify common themes.

3. Say: **Family-school meetings actually solve problems without blame and make participants feel hopeful about each other and the child's prospects for learning and growth.**

Activity II. Introduction

INSTRUCTIONS

1. Say: **At the core of successful problem-solving meetings is the set of sequential steps, a "meeting flow" sequence of skills to which you have already been introduced. We are going to review these steps in depth since in these often-tense meetings their effective use makes the difference between success and failure.**

2. Distribute *Collaborative Meeting Flow Steps: Introduction* Handout #1 to participants. Ask them to read it to themselves and then briefly review the steps with them and explain that today we are going to focus on the *Introduction* or *Overview* to a problem-solving meeting.

3. Explain that chairs should be arranged in a circle with no one sitting behind a desk or with tables between them.

4. Say: **Each meeting begins with an introduction or overview, which serves two purposes: FIRST, it introduces all participants to each other and identifies their position in the school, family, or relationship to the school or family. SECOND, it sets a tone that reassures the child, parent and teachers:**

- **That this is not a punishment meeting,**
- **That blame will be blocked in this meeting, and**
- **That the goal of the meeting is for all of the participants to reach consensus about critical concerns and to develop a collaborative plan for solving the problem that everyone will feel good about.**

5. Distribute *Examples of Introductions* Handout #2 and *Steps to Our Family-School Problem-Solving Meeting* Handout #3. Ask participants to review the examples and comment on them. Additionally, ask them if any aspects of the introductions confuse them or seem uncomfortable for them. Make sure to highlight the language used in *Steps to Our Family-School Problem-Solving Meeting* and explain that this could be used to introduce the process to people unfamiliar with it.

6. *Think about it.* Pose the following questions to participants:

- *What would it be like for a child to hear a meeting framed like this versus one of the encounters you described above from your own past?*

- *How do you think the child would feel about participating in the meeting after hearing one of these introductions?*

Activity III. Role Play

INSTRUCTIONS

1. Ask participants to form groups of five or six (depending on the age of their students) and role-play introductions for meetings in their own words and style. They are to take turns being the Facilitator. Each Facilitator should practice the introduction, get feedback from the group, and if need be try the introduction again.

2. Give participants about 10-15 minutes to do the role-plays. Then ask them how they did with the introductions and ask them if they have any questions or comments about introducing a family-school meeting.

SESSION 16
Handout 1

Collaborative Meeting Flow Steps: Introduction

1. Introduction - The purpose and tone of the meeting are established. Participants are assured that this is a non-blaming, non-punishment meeting and that the goal of the meeting is to develop a plan with which everyone agrees.

↓

2. Finding Facts - This stage identifies the key issues as participants see them. Each person is asked to state his/her one or two chief concerns. The Facilitator starts with the school staff, asking the principal and then the teacher and support personnel to share their chief concerns. Then the Facilitator questions the family about their concerns. Paying attention to the family hierarchy, he/she questions the parents first, and then the siblings and the child with the identified problem.

↓

3. Blocking Blame - While finding facts, the leader blocks blame thereby creating a non-blaming atmosphere. The purpose of the meeting is not to establish blame or decide who or what 'caused' the problem but to use the shared energy of the group to solve the problem.

↓

4. Checking for Consensus - Participants identify the primary topics and/or themes that emerge from finding facts and agree on issues to work on. The leader ascertains that people have a common sense of the definition of the problem.

↓

5. Determining a Decision - The group decides on what issues that will be addressed in this meeting. It is made clear which issues they will not make decisions about in this meeting. They determine what if anything should be done to develop a plan to solve the problem. This decision becomes the standard of measure against which to evaluate progress or change.

↓

6. Arriving at Action - The group develops a final plan. The child, the parents, school staff and relevant others jointly agree on what specific actions they will take including who will do what, how, when, and where. Group determines a plan for follow-up.

SESSION 16
Handout 2

Examples of Introductions to Family-School Meetings

Typical Introduction for Early Elementary School Child

Hello, I'd like to welcome everyone to this meeting. We are all here to help things go better for Sally. Let's go around and introduce ourselves. My name is (*Dr. Valdez*) and I'm the (*school principal.*)

(*After the introductions, turn to the child.*) Sally, I know it might be a little uncomfortable and confusing to you to be here with so many grown-ups. I want you to understand that all of these grown-ups are here just to help you. This is not a punishment meeting and it's not a blaming meeting. No one is going to scold you or yell at you. In fact we'd really like to hear from you because you can help us understand how things are going for you in school. We want to hear from each other while we are all together, so we can understand any problems. We have lots of ways to help you. Okay? Do you have any questions?

We're here to help Sally. Together, we're going to come up with a family-school plan for Sally. I'd like to hear from each of you about what your primary concerns are about Sally. *(To child)* Sally, do you know what concerns are? Concerns are things that make people worried or sad or mad. Let's go around the room again and begin with Mr. R, Sally's teacher. Mr. R what are your one or two main concerns about how Sally is doing in school?

Typical Introduction to a Middle Elementary School Child

I'd like to welcome all of you to this meeting. We've all come together to find ways of helping Johnny have a more successful year. Let's go around the room and introduce ourselves. I'm (*Mary Smith*), the coordinator of this meeting and the (*school guidance counselor*) [*everyone introduces themselves one by one*]. I want to be clear about something and that is that this meeting is about helping Johnny, not about blaming anyone. *[Talk directly to child]* Johnny, I really want you to understand that this is not a punishment meeting. All of these adults are here because they care about you and want things to go better.

We're here to help Johnny. I'd like to hear your primary concerns about Johnny from each of you. Then, together, we will come up with a family-school plan for Johnny. *[To child]* Johnny, we really need to hear from you. You are the world's expert on you. Only you can help us understand what you are thinking or feeling about your experiences and how we can help you. Let's go around the room again and begin with Mrs. K, Johnny's teacher. Mrs. K, what are your one or two main concerns about Johnny?

Typical Introduction for Secondary School Student

We're here to discuss how things are going in school for Henry. We'll discuss how things are going and what concerns people have. Then we'll come up with a plan to help things go better for Henry. Let's introduce ourselves first. I am Sam Gould, the school social worker and family-school coordinator. *[Others introduce themselves].*

Now that we've all met, I want to hear from everyone first about their main concerns. Then we'll decide on a plan together to help Henry.

Before we begin I want to make it clear that the purpose of this meeting is not to criticize Henry or get him into trouble. We're here to understand how things are going and to find a way to help things go better in school for Henry. *[Turn to student]* Henry, you may be worried that everyone's upset with you and will come down hard on you. This is not a blaming meeting or a punishment meeting. We're here so everyone including you can express their concerns and come up with a plan. And it's real important that we hear from you. You know more about yourself and your situation than anyone else in this room and only you can tell us what's going on and what might work. Okay, first, I'd like to hear from Henry's homeroom and major subject teachers. Mr. J, will you begin please? What are your one or two main concerns about Henry?

SESSION 16
Handout 3

Steps to Our Family-School Problem-Solving Meeting

Our goal today is to work together to explore the problem and develop a plan that will help your child have more success in school.

Here are the steps we'll go through:

INTRODUCTION: Everyone will introduce him/herself. The meeting Facilitator will explain the purpose of the meeting and how the meeting will be organized.

FINDING FACTS: Each person will have a chance to discuss his or her one or two main concerns about the child in school. The teacher will also have a chance to talk about what is going well for the child.

BLOCKING BLAME: Blame is not productive for anyone at the meeting, and we all need to work to block blame of ourselves and others.

CHECKING FOR CONSENSUS: We will identify areas of agreement in people's concerns about the child.

DETERMINING A DECISION: The group will agree to work on one or two areas and develop a plan.

ARRIVING AT ACTION: Together we will develop a plan that specifies what each participant, including the child, will do.

FOLLOW-UP MEETING: We will have a follow-up meeting between two to four weeks after today's meeting. In the follow-up meeting, we will discuss how the plan was implemented, its effectiveness in helping the child, and what further steps or modifications are needed to help the child continue to improve.

End of Session 16

SESSION 17: How can the meeting flow steps be tailored to family-school problem-solving meetings?

Rationale:

In each of the following two sessions, participants will be presented with the same three case vignettes. These will become the focus of their efforts to tailor the sequence of meeting flow steps for family-school meetings. Once they have worked extensively with these examples, they will be ready to apply their newly acquired skills to the issues they confront in their work environments.

Goals

- To practice using specific meeting flow steps within the context of family-school problem-solving meetings.
- To simulate the step of finding facts in a problem-solving meeting.
- To hone skills in blocking blame through role-plays of potentially tense or angry situations.

Handouts/Materials

- *Finding Facts*
- *Case Examples*
- *Techniques for Blocking Blame*
- *Collaborative Meeting Flow Steps: First Three Steps*
- *Feedback Sheet for Finding Facts*
- White board/Smart Board or chart paper

Introduction

Say: Last time we explored ways to begin and offer overviews of family-school problem-solving meetings. Today we are going to focus on the Finding Facts stage of the meeting flow steps in family-school meetings. We will also explore ways to block blame so these meetings can proceed towards a constructive plan. We will actually role-play the beginning stages of a meeting.

Activity I. Finding Facts

INSTRUCTIONS

1. **Say: The primary objective of this step is to convey a clear picture of the concerns that all participants (including the student) have about the student's school experience. Highlighting the student's strengths is very important so that the participants understand the child as a whole person and not just in relation to particular difficulties.**

2. Distribute *Finding Facts* Handout #1. Have participants read it over, and remind them of the following guidelines:

- Set priorities with students for whom there are numerous areas of concern. It is especially important that only one or two critical concerns are selected for discussion. A very useful question to ask all participants to start "finding facts" is: "What is your primary concern" or "What are your two most important concerns".
- Make sure *everyone* (including the child) in the meeting is asked about their primary concerns.
- Have individuals describe the child's or other's behaviors in observable (behavioral) terms. Avoid describing character traits; ask participants to describe what people do. Rather than saying Johnny is "aggressive," it is more useful to say "when Johnny does not get his way on the playground, he pushes and yells at the other boys."
- Give the context of the behavior. There are four contexts to consider: social, activity, time of day, and historical.

Questions to ask within these contexts include:

- With who does this behavior occur?
- Are there particular subjects or activities where this behavior is seen most often? In what circumstances are you least likely to see this behavior?
- Is there a particular time of day that seems more or less problematic?
- When did the problem begin?
- Have you seen any changes over time?
- When does this behavior not occur?

Activity II. Blocking Blame

INSTRUCTIONS

1. Review the previous discussion and exercises about blocking blame with participants.

2. Distribute *Case Examples* Handout #2 and *Techniques for Blocking Blame* Handout #3. Have participants review both.

3. Say: **Now pair up with a partner. Review the three vignettes in the Case Examples handout and discuss how individuals in family-school meetings in the three examples might blame each other. For instance, in example 3 the mother might say to the assistant principal: "If you people were doing your job right, you'd know where the kids are and you'd be able to get them to go to classes instead of dragging the parents in."**

4. Have the pairs report out, sharing types of blaming statements that could be said in each of the vignettes and how you would block blame and refocus to a problem-solving perspective.

Activity III. Role-Play

INSTRUCTIONS

1. Break participants into three groups and assign each group one of the examples on the *Case Examples* handout to role-play. They are to determine who is to play each role and assign those who are not assuming a role to be observers.

2. Distribute *Collaborative Meeting Flow Steps: First Three Steps* Handout #4 to each group. Ask each group to role-play the first three steps of the meeting flow sequence: Introduction, Finding Facts, and Blocking Blame.

3. Observe the groups to make sure they do not jump from fact finding to offering explanations and/or problem resolution.

4. In preparation for the next session, have the 'reporter' record primary concerns of each participant and hand them in to you. Record which participants are in which role-play.

5. Using *Feedback Sheet for Finding Facts* Handout #5, ask participants to share their experiences in each of the groups from perspectives of Facilitators, parents, student, teacher and other school staff.

6. Summarize difficulties and other notable responses on chart paper.

7. Ask the group to identify common problems/concerns that emerge. Lead a discussion of ways to address these problems.

SESSION 17
Handout 1

Finding Facts

Issues

- The "facts" are the actions, thoughts, and feelings that the participants report. This information provides the basis from which consensus among participants is reached and a collaborative solution to the problem is developed.
- The step of finding facts consists of each person reporting his or her concerns about the student or the situation. The Facilitator probes to highlight these concerns but also to put them in a context that includes the child's strengths.
- The teacher's report serves as a model for others and follows these criteria:

    1. Set priorities-select the two or three most important things to focus on.
    2. Describe actions.
    3. Give context of observed actions.
    4. Use language the child and family understand.
    5. Be direct-don't pull punches.

Examples

1. Set priorities and be direct:

    "There are two things that I'm most concerned about. The first is John's pattern of lateness to school. The second is a change I've observed in how John responds to assignments. He does not give much effort to learning tasks. "

2. Describe actions and use language the child and family understands:

    "For the last three weeks, John has been late to school nine times. [Have the attendance book there.] I've noticed what looks to me like a very sad expression on his face most of the time. He walks heavily and his posture is slumped. "

3. Give context of observed actions:

    "This is different from the way John was in school before. He's never had a lateness problem. He used to respond to school with what looked to me like a lot of energy and enthusiasm. He worked very hard on his assignments. "

SESSION 17
Handout 2

Case Examples

Example 1

Parents who are recent immigrants to the USA from the Dominican Republic and have never been to parent-school conferences are asked to attend a meeting to deal with their son's aggressive acting-out behavior in the classroom and the lunchroom. Present are the child's teacher, the guidance counselor, the assistant principal who will translate for the parents, the child and the Facilitator. Parents are confused and angry about the different rules regarding corporal punishment in the US compared to the Dominican Republic. The teacher is worried that the parents may be punishing the boy too harshly.

Example 2

The parents of a kindergarten student have been asked to attend a family-school problem-solving meeting, because the child cries every time her mother leaves her at school, and then intermittently during the school day whenever she is confused or upset. According to the girl's mother, she and her daughter's father are undergoing an amicable divorce. The mother brings the child to school every day and sometimes volunteers in the classroom. The father has only been to school to attend parent-teacher conferences. At the meeting are the girl, her mother, her father, the teacher and the guidance counselor who facilitates the meeting. The teacher thinks the mother is overwhelmed and overprotective of the child and that the father is under-involved with his daughter.

Example 3

The parents of a high school junior are asked to attend a family-school problem-solving meeting to address their daughter's chronic cutting of classes and declining grades. Present at the conference are the parents, their daughter, the assistant principal, and the guidance counselor who runs the meeting. The school staff believes that the girl's father is an alcoholic. Her mother has a reputation with the teachers of being hostile and uncooperative.

SESSION 17
Handout 3

Techniques for Blocking Blame

DIRECT BLOCKING - Signaling that the purpose of the interaction is not to blame but to solve a problem.

    EXAMPLE: **Student:** Johnny always starts the fights -- it's not my fault.

                         Teacher: We're not here to find out who's to blame, but to figure out how you and Johnny can get your work done instead of fighting.

REFRAMING - Providing an alternative point of view about a set of facts which gives the facts a more positive, productive meaning.

    EXAMPLE: **Teacher:** She gets the other girls in trouble by getting them to break the rules.

                         Principal: It sounds like other girls view Quiana as a leader. We need to help direct her leadership potential in more appropriate ways.

PROBING - Eliciting additional information to clarify the context leading to the blaming.

    EXAMPLE: **Student:** You (the teacher) always pick on me.

                         Teacher: I certainly don't intend to pick on you, David. What do you see me doing that makes you think I'm picking on you? Give me some examples.

REFOCUSING - A statement which redirects the discussion from a non-productive or nonessential area to an area relevant to helping the student.

    EXAMPLE: **Mother:** Derrick's father was always getting into trouble at school and had never finished school himself.

                         Teacher: What do you think makes it difficult for Derrick to do well in school?

ILLUSTRATING - Giving concrete examples of areas of concern.

    EXAMPLE: **Parent:** She doesn't act that way at home. You just don't know how to deal with her.

        Teacher: What I've observed is that Mary acts that way when she is with her friends. They enjoy talking with each other so much that they don't seem to be able to stop when it's time to get down to work.

VALIDATING - Recognizing the validity of another's perceptions or efforts.

    EXAMPLE: **Teacher:** You know, Jose takes up so much of my time and attention I don't have much left over to give to any other child in the class.

        Parent: I understand that with 30 children in the classroom there are lots of demands on your time and attention.

AGREEING - Confirming someone's perception of a situation.

    EXAMPLE: **Teacher:** It really drives me nuts when parents come in to my classroom without any notice and assume they can interrupt as they please. We need more structure in our visiting policies. I don't want them to expect I will drop everything to talk to them.

        Principal: Giving more structure to our visiting policy might be helpful. I can see how it would enable you to be more at ease about how to engage parents in classroom activities if you could anticipate their visits or establish regular routines for their involvements.

SESSION 17
Handout 4

Collaborative Meeting Flow Steps: First Three Steps

1. Introduction - The purpose and tone of the meeting are established. Participants are assured that this is a non-blaming, non-punishment meeting and that the goal of the meeting is to develop a plan with which everyone agrees.

↓

2. Finding Facts - This stage identifies the key issues as participants see them. Each person is asked to state his/her one or two chief concerns. The Facilitator starts with the school staff, asking the principal and then the teacher and support personnel to share their chief concerns. Then the Facilitator questions the family about their concerns. Paying attention to the family hierarchy, he/she questions the parents first, and then the siblings and the child with the identified problem.

↓

3. Blocking Blame - While finding facts, the leader blocks blame thereby creating a non-blaming atmosphere. The purpose of the meeting is not to establish blame or decide who or what 'caused' the problem but to use the shared energy of the group to solve the problem.

↓

4. Checking for Consensus - Participants identify the primary topics and/or themes that emerge from finding facts and agree on issues to work on. The leader ascertains that people have a common sense of the definition of the problem.

↓

5. Determining a Decision - The group decides on what issues will be addressed in this meeting. It makes clear which issues they will not make decisions about in this meeting. They determine what if anything should be done to develop a plan to solve the problem. This decision becomes the standard of measure against which to evaluate progress or change.

↓

6. Arriving at Action - The group develops a final plan. The child, the parents, school staff and significant others jointly agree on what specific actions they will take including who will do what, how, when, and where. The group determines a plan for follow-up.

SESSION 17
Handout 5

Feedback Sheet for Finding Facts

From the Facilitator's Perspective:

- What was the most difficult aspect of Finding Facts?
- How hard was it to find facts without moving to problem solving? Who had the most difficulty? Systemically, how would you explain this? How did you handle it?
- Did you get sufficient information?
- Did you learn anything you might not have if the child were not present?

From the Parents' Perspective:

- Was the purpose of the meeting clear?
- Did you learn anything new about the school and/or about your child's experience there?
- How do you feel you were treated? Did you feel heard?

For the Student:

- Was the meeting what you expected or different? How was it different?
- How do you feel you were treated? Did you feel heard?
- How did you feel about being at the meeting by the end of the Finding Facts?

For the Teacher/School Staff:

- Did you feel heard at the meeting?
- Were your concerns taken seriously?
- Did you learn anything you might not have if the child had not been present?
- Did anyone in the role-play feel blamed?
- Was anyone especially blaming? How successfully was blame blocked?
- In retrospect, what else might have been done to block blame?

End of Session 17

SESSION 18: What do the last three steps of a family-school problem-solving meeting look like?

Rationale:

It is important for participants to review the final three meeting flow steps in the specific context of the *family-school problem solving meetings* where the anticipation of tension and anger may be great. Having the opportunity to practice the techniques in this session will allow participants to better anticipate and prepare for appropriate and effective ways to facilitate actual meetings. This session, like the last one, will review these critical skills.

Goals

- To practice skills of checking for consensus in a family-school meeting.
- To increase the ability to determine a decision about the specific problem at hand at this meeting.
- To formulate an action plan that various constituents will be responsible for and determine follow-up procedures.

Handouts/Materials

- *Checking for Consensus, Determining a Decision and Arriving at Action*
- *Case Examples*
- *Sample Latent Themes*
- *Family-School Conference Summary Form*
- White board/Smart Board or chart paper

Introduction

Say: **This is the final workshop session in which we will tailor the Collaborative Meeting Flow Steps to Family-School Problem-Solving Meetings. Today we will explore and role-play the last three critical steps of the Meeting Flow Sequence: Checking for Consensus, Determining a Decision, and Arriving at Action. These three steps help the group come to an agreement about what issue they will address and devise a plan for dealing with this issue. The three steps determine the success of the meeting's outcome: whether or not people come away thinking that something useful, do-able and constructive has been accomplished.**

Activity I. Lecture/Discussion on Stages of Family-School Problem-Solving Meeting

INSTRUCTIONS

1. Say: **We will begin the session with a quick review of the last three stages specifically as they apply to the Family-School Problem-Solving Meeting format.**

Checking for Consensus

First is Checking for Consensus. There are two components to this stage. The first is identifying Manifest Themes. The Facilitator of the meeting needs to feed back to the group the topics (i.e. behavioral issues) or manifest themes which surfaced in the meeting and about which there seems to be shared concern. The purpose is to see if everyone agrees that these are the most important themes to be addressed. For example in Case Example 2 from our last session, the manifest behavior the group may agree on is the girl's crying. Here is the example again (have participants review in their binder, or read the following):

> **Example 2**
>
> The parents of a kindergarten student who cries every time her mother leaves her at school, and then intermittently during the school day whenever she is confused or upset, are asked to attend a family-school meeting. According to the girl's mother, she and her daughter's father are undergoing an amicable divorce. The mother is at school daily with the girl; however the father has only been there once to attend a parent-teacher conference. At the meeting are the girl, her mother, her father, the teacher, and the guidance counselor who facilitates the meeting. The teacher thinks the mother is overwhelmed and overprotective of the child and that the father is under-involved with his daughter.

2. Distribute *Sample Latent Themes* Handout #3.

3. Say: **The second component of checking for consensus is identifying latent themes. These are less apparent overarching themes, which may include several manifest topics simultaneously. For instance in Example 2 above the latent theme may be the girl's struggle to deal with two difficult new situations simultaneously: the beginning of elementary school and**

the separation of her parents. In response to these two events, she may be fearful and worried about her mother. It is important that the Facilitator choose a theme that will have the most impact for shifting the relationships in the group.

This is done by selecting a theme that:

- Allows people to be seen in a different light that will lead to positive change.
- Provides the group with hope instead of a renewed adversarial relationship.
- Is a positive, rather than blaming and toxic, way of talking about the issue.
- Opens up more options for intervention.

4. *Think about it.* Ask participants to reflect on the following:

- *Does the theme of the girl's facing new situations and her concern about her mother meet the criteria I've just listed?*

5. Go down list of criteria and see if this reframe matches. Say: **In the example above, the situation rather than the child becomes the focus for discussion. The girl is seen as caring and concerned rather than merely meek and frightened. In other words, what was previously seen as a weakness can be viewed as an area of strength.**

Using this theme opens more options for the child for two reasons:

1. She is seen as competent in certain areas, and a plan can build on these strengths to help her address her worries.
2. It situates the issues in the broader context of home and school.

<u>Determining a Decision</u>

6. Say: **Let's move on to the next step-- determining a decision. The goal of this step is for the group to decide specifically what issues/behaviors (topics or themes) they want to address in a plan. Their focus may be the most severe behavior or it may be the behavior that, if changed would have the greatest effect on other problem behaviors. Thus helping a student get to school on time may be selected as the focus before dealing with what actually happens in school.**

In determining a decision:

- The child should always have an action in the plan.
- The focus of the plan should be on school-related issues.

- The plan should in some way include the student, teacher and the parents.
- The plan should be appropriate for the roles and positions of the participants.
- The plan should be appropriate for the skill level of the participants.

In the example we used above, the group might decide to focus on the girl's concerns about her mother and the newness of kindergarten instead of directly addressing her crying. They might decide to design a plan to reassure the girl that both she and her mother are safe, and that her father is interested in her school life too. Giving the girl an opportunity to describe the things she likes about kindergarten to the adults may refocus everyone to an area to which they can all contribute.

Arriving at Action

7. **Say:** The goal of this step is to develop a concrete plan. The plan is a new beginning and needs to concretely specify:

- **Who:** Who will do the tasks?
- **What:** What will the tasks be?
- **When:** At what times and how often will the tasks be done?
- **How:** What do people expect of themselves and each other in carrying out the plan? How will they do what they do?
- **Follow-Up:** How and when will the plan be evaluated? What follow-up steps will be taken including scheduling a follow-up meeting?

It is essential that a feedback loop be built into the plan so that everyone knows what everyone else is expected to do and when.

If possible the plan should be written up and distributed to all the participants before the meeting adjourns.

Activity II. Brainstorming a Plan

INSTRUCTIONS

1. Ask participants to brainstorm possible components of a plan for the kindergarten child discussed above.

2. List these on the board. Discuss their feasibility and how well they meet the criteria outlined above.

3. Discuss how the group would follow-up the plan they have developed. A follow-up meeting is often very useful to cement the more collaborative relations family members and school staff have achieved. It also is useful for making clear that their ongoing partnership can be used to insure the success of the child (not just problem-solve meetings).

Some possibilities include:

> - The girl and her mother devise a parting ritual that they perform each morning when they leave the house and when the mother leaves the girl at school.
> - Each time the girl feels worried about her mother she can signal the teacher who will signal back to indicate that she will listen and try to help her refocus on something interesting in school as soon as she can.
> - The girl's father will check in with her each evening to hear about her day and talk with her especially about her non-worry, non-crying activities in school.

Activity III. Role Play of the Final Three Meeting Flow Steps

INSTRUCTIONS

1. Divide participants into two groups. Assign each group one of the following examples. Make sure that the groups for each example are composed primarily of people who dealt with that example during the previous session. People who worked with the example of the kindergarten girl can be reassigned to other groups.

2. Explain that the groups are to conduct a role-play of the final three stages of the family-school problem-solving meeting for their examples, i.e. checking for consensus, determining a decision and arriving at action. They are to use the information they generated in the finding facts role-play as the basis for their continued discussion.

3. Distribute *Family-School Conference Summary Form* Handout #4 and instruct them to complete this as part of the role-play.

4. Give each group 15 minutes to do the role-play.

5. Have groups share their plans and the process by which they derived them.

6. Discuss the participants' reactions to the role-play experience and the reports of the group plans. Consider the clarity and specificity of each plan.

7. Remind participants: **Note that in a follow-up to an initial family-school problem-solving meeting, participants may not have completed a task they were supposed to do. It is important that the group maintain a non-blaming stance. If a plan does not work, we take the stance that it was a lousy plan. If it were a good enough plan, we would have anticipated difficulties in doing it. Consider what things were perhaps not addressed adequately by the first plan. For example, the teacher may have offered to do some things in the spirit of teamwork, but later discovered that she just did not have the time. A revised plan should realistically deal with time demands. It is important to keep the problem-solving group focused on achieving the desired change rather than on its disappointment that a plan did not have immediate results.**

Activity IV. Reflection of Meeting Flow Steps (Optional)

INSTRUCTIONS

1. Ask the groups to discuss those aspects of the meeting flow which they found most difficult and record their observations on newsprint. Identify common themes and discuss the elements that make these aspects of the meetings especially difficult. Request volunteers to role-play these specific steps.

SESSION 18
Handout 1

Checking for Consensus, Determining a Decision and Arriving at Action

Checking for Consensus

Primary guideline- Identify the topic or thematic focus that will have the most impact for shifting the relationships in the group on toward ongoing collaborative partnership. This is done by selecting a theme that:

- Allows people to be seen in a different light that will lead to a positive change.
- Provides the group with hope rather than with a renewed adversarial relationship.
- Is a positive rather than blaming or toxic way of talking about the issue or concern.
- Opens up more options for intervention.

Determining a Decision

- The child should always have an action to do in the plan.
- The focus of the plan should be on school-related issues. Focus on family interaction at home must be specifically legitimized by parents as helpful and related to school-based concerns.
- The plan should in some way include the student, teacher, and parents.
- The plan should be appropriate for the roles and positions of the participants.
- The plan should be appropriate for the skill level of the participants.

Arriving at Action

- Who - *who* will do the task?
- What - *what* will the tasks be?
- When - by *when* will the tasks be done?
- How - *how* will participants do what they do? What is the standard of quality for doing the tasks?
- Follow-up - *how* will the plan be evaluated?

SESSION 18
Handout 2

Case Examples

Example 1

Parents who are recent immigrants to the USA from the Dominican Republic and have never been to parent-school conferences are asked to attend a meeting to deal with their son's aggressive acting out behavior in the classroom and the lunchroom. Present are the child's teacher, the guidance counselor, the assistant principal who will translate for the parents, the child and the facilitator. Parents are confused and angry about the different rules regarding corporal punishment in the US compared to the Dominican Republic. The teacher is worried that the parents may be punishing the boy too harshly.

Example 2

The parents of a kindergarten student have been asked to attend a family-school problem-solving meeting because the child cries every time her mother leaves her at school and then intermittently during the school day whenever she is confused or upset. According to the girl's mother, she and her daughter's father are undergoing an amicable divorce. The mother brings the child to school every day and sometimes volunteers in the classroom. The father has only been to school to attend parent-teacher conferences. At the meeting are the girl, her mother, her father, the teacher, and the guidance counselor who facilitates the meeting. The teacher thinks the mother is overwhelmed and overprotective of the child and that the father is under involved with his daughter.

Example 3

The parents of a high school junior are asked to attend a family-school problem-solving meeting to address their daughter's chronic cutting of classes and declining grades. Present at the conference are the parents, their daughter, the assistant principal, and the guidance counselor who runs the meeting. The school staff believes that the girl's father is an alcoholic. Her mother has a reputation with the teachers of being hostile and uncooperative.

SESSION 18
Handout 3

Sample Latent Themes

1. Autonomy/independence vs. parental authority

2. Being valued

3. Being accepted

4. Building social connections *(e.g., child-child, parent-parent, parent-teacher, teacher-child, teacher-teacher)*

5. Clarity of expectations

6. Building courage

7. Fairness

8. "Hangover" effect in making transitions

9. Lack of satisfaction images -- building satisfaction images

10. Maintaining individual integrity under group pressure

11. Newness panic

12. Reputation

13. Respect

14. Responsibility-taking *(e.g., teaming to do what you dislike doing)*

15. Risking success, failure and mistakes

16. Shifting complementary of roles *(one-up/one-down, giver-receiver)*

17. Skill building

18. Sociological/ethnic taste patterns (family, school, peer group) *(e.g., discipline norms)*

19. Temptation resistance

SESSION 18
Handout 4

Family-School Conference Summary Form

Student: **Grade:**

Attendees:

Led by:

Reason for Meeting:

Problems to Work On:

Plan:

Signed by Student: _____   **Next Meeting:**

Signed by Parent: _____   **Date:**
                                                                                            Time:

End of Session 18

SESSION 19: How do we implement a successful problem-solving meeting for multiple families?

Rationale:

So far, we have explored problem-solving meetings organized for one family at a time. However, this versatile format can also be adapted for use with several families at once. Families whose children share a common problem can come together to discuss concerns and develop plans. This format can not only help to normalize the problems that students are experiencing, but also can be a highly effective force in motivating families to act – sometimes jointly – on their children's behalf. In this session, we will examine an actual multiple family problem-solving meeting that was convened for parents and students of an alternative high school. Participants will follow each step of the meeting, have the opportunity to gauge its effectiveness, and discuss their reactions.

Goals

- To understand how the meeting flow steps can be applied to a multiple family-school problem-solving meeting.

- To formulate hypothetical action plans and follow-up procedures for various constituents in an actual multi-family problem-solving meeting.

- To reflect on the potential effectiveness of multiple family-school problem-solving meetings.

Handouts/Materials

- *Case Example: Alternate School*
- *Sample Multiple Family Problem-Solving List: Alternate School*
- White board/Smart Board or chart paper

Introduction

Say: **We've already spent some time exploring what a problem-solving meeting might look like for one child and his or her family. But sometimes, you might find it a powerful tool to group together families that are in a similar position and discuss how to best move forward to improve that position. We can use our problem-solving skills to help us brainstorm a plan in this case. Today, we'll spend some time working with materials from an**

actual multiple family problem-solving meeting. You will have the opportunity to work with issues the participants raised and begin to formulate hypothetical plans.

Activity I. Case Example

INSTRUCTIONS

1. Distribute *Case Example: Alternate School* Handout #1. Ask participants to read through it and ask any questions they might have about the situation.

2. Say: **Now, let's see what the groups at this actual meeting came up with.**

3. Distribute *Sample Multiple Family Problem-Solving Meeting List* Handout #2. Ask participants to read through the lists.

Activity II. Developing a Plan

INSTRUCTIONS

1. Break participants into groups with three or four members in each group. Ask them to use their Final Three Meeting Flow Steps knowledge and handouts to write down a plan of addressing at least one of the issues raised by the families. Be sure to remind participants of critical ingredients of the final steps of a meeting:

> - A clear focus for collaboration on a specific problem.
> - A role for everyone at the meeting in the plan.
> - Specific, concrete language about who does what, with whom, how often, when and where.
> - A set time to follow-up on the plan and determine if it has succeeded.

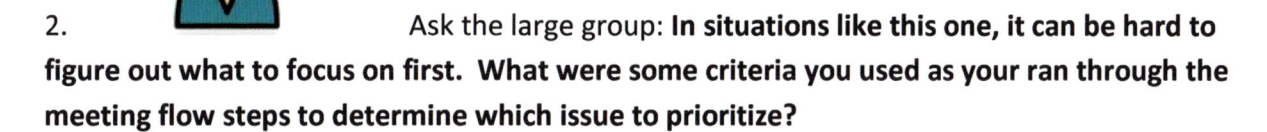

2. Ask the large group: **In situations like this one, it can be hard to figure out what to focus on first. What were some criteria you used as your ran through the meeting flow steps to determine which issue to prioritize?**

3. Record responses on chart paper.

Activity III. Reflection

INSTRUCTIONS

1. *Think about it.* Reconvene the large group and ask the following:

   - *Can you foresee the use for a multiple family problem-solving meeting in your school? If so, in which situations?*

   - *What are some of the challenges you can foresee for working with multiple families as opposed to families of one individual child?*

SESSION 19

Handout 1

Case Example: Alternate School

A multiple-family problem-solving meeting consisting of students, their families, teachers and support personnel in a suburban alternative high school is convened. The school, consisting of 35 students and 2 teachers, was a 'last stop' for students who were in danger of being expelled from the system. Housed in a remote building on the local high school campus, this school served students who had been ejected from the main high school building as a result of chronic absenteeism, failure, acting out behavior, and social and emotional problems.

The teachers and support personnel who provided services to the students felt that if the school was to succeed they had to set a new tone and enlist the help of students' families.

The staff wanted help in transforming the school's identity from a place for losers to a place for hope. Aware that parents' previous experiences with the school were predominantly negative -- threats, ultimatums and notices of failure -- teachers knew that they had to send a very different message to parents if they were going to enlist their support. They invited parents and students to attend 'Night at the Alternate' requesting their help in improving the school.

A record number of parents attended the meeting. At the meeting, small groups of parents and students (not necessarily parents and their own children) discussed things that go well at the alternate school and things that concerned them or needed improvement. The large group reconvened and two lists (of things that go well and things needing improvement) were created as small groups reported out. These lists were then grouped thematically and the group decided which one of two issues it wanted to work on at the present time. Plans were then formulated for these issues.

SESSION 19
Handout 2

Sample Multiple-Family Problem-Solving Meeting List

Things that Go Well at the Alternate

- Small classes
- Individual pace
- Patience with the students
- Teachers/support staff care about the students
- Students have a second chance
- Individual attention
- Good teachers
- Fewer rules than in the main building
- Shorter school day than in the main building
- Teachers try to help students and parents
- Improved attendance
- No competition

Concerns and Things Needing Improvement

- Need better idea of how vocational education fits into the Alternate
- Students feel cut off from the main building
- How can parents/teachers help students understand the value of education
- Students are left out of activities in the main building
- Students feel there is a negative stigma associated with attending the Alternate
- Students need to get a clearer sense of the goals for their education and their future
- Students need to understand what colleges/vocational schools they can attend after the Alternate
- Students don't know what's going on in the main building
- Students want to change rules about smoking
- Teachers in the main building don't seem to care about the Alternate students

Section 5

Elective Climate Building:
New Opportunities for Collaboration

SESSION 20: How do we review issues in our school from a collaborative point of view?

Rationale:

Once schools experience the power of family-school collaboration, they recognize its potential as a resource for achieving their objectives and addressing their specific needs. Elective climate-building activities make each school's family-school collaboration program unique.

Goals

- To understand roles that parents can play in collaborative work.
- To brainstorm ideas for elective climate-building activities.
- To introduce specific examples of climate-building activities as models for planning.

Handouts/Materials

- *Parent Roles*
- *Sample Elective Climate-Building Activities*
- *Multiple Perspective Form*

Introduction

Say: **So far we have experienced the planning and implementing of core collaborative activities. In this session we are going to begin exploring how to develop elective activities geared specifically to the unique needs of your school.**

Activity I. Exploring Parents' Roles

INSTRUCTIONS

1. Distribute *Parents' Roles* Handout #1. Instruct participants to take 5 minutes to complete the handout, indicating school activities that parents are engaged in for each role.

2. *Think about it.* After participants have completed the form, have them reflect on the following:

- *For which roles were you able to come up with the most descriptions of school activities?*

- *For which roles were you able to conceive of only a few or none?*

- *Why do you think that these particular roles have so many fewer activities?*

Activity II. Identifying Elective Climate-Building Activities

INSTRUCTIONS

1. Distribute *Sample Elective Climate-Building Activities* Handout #2. Give participants five minutes to read through, and ask for any feedback.

2. Break into school-based small groups.

3. Say: **In your groups, please identify an issue that could be addressed in your school through a collaborative conversation, or an already-existing social event such as multi-cultural night that you would like to make more collaborative. Please use the questions on your handout as guidelines for planning, and remember the importance of tying collaborative climate-building activities to substantive issues such as curriculum or assessment, as well as social events such as family-school dinners, picnics, and fund-raising events.**

Also, keep in mind that the findings of the needs assessment questionnaire you completed can be a way to prioritize issues – what did respondents see as the biggest need?

You can also apply the four components of climate – culture, milieu, social system and ecology – as a guide for choosing your issue – is there an issue that touches on all four components?

Next time, we'll plan the actual event; today, just focus on the issue that your event will target.

Allow groups to work for at least 15 minutes.

Activity III. Multiple Perspectives

INSTRUCTIONS

1. Allot 10 to 15 minutes for participants to share the issues they've identified with the rest of the group and obtain feedback.

2. Distribute *Multiple Perspectives Form* Handout #3.

3. *Think about it.* Ask those listening to reflect on the multiple perspectives form and the following as groups present:

- *Is this issue presented to staff, families and children in a non-blaming way?*

- *How much interest is there in this issue at school?*

- *How can we alternatively frame the issue to gain wider interest and engagement from families?*

- *How can we send a message to parents that their participation in this event will contribute positively to their own children's school experience*

SESSION 20

Handout 1

Parent Roles

1. **Parents as partners, e.g., doing joint assignments with children:**

   ACTIVITIES _____

   _____

   _____

2. **Parents as collaborators and problem solvers, e.g. meeting with school staff to plan how to help a child:**

   ACTIVITIES _____

   _____

   _____

3. **Parents as audience, e.g., coming for assemblies:**

   ACTIVITIES _____

   _____

   _____

4. **Parents as supporters, e.g., tutoring, chaperoning:**

   ACTIVITIES _____

   _____

   _____

5. **Parents as advisors and/or co-decision makers, e.g., school-based management team:**

   ACTIVITIES _____

   _____

   _____

SESSION 20
Handout 2

Sample Elective Climate-Building Activities

The following examples highlight how a collaborative approach can help expand parent roles. It is important to broaden the definition of family involvement from taking part in a series of "individual events" to a more substantive role, reflecting a shift in the way climate-building activities are organized, how they are carried out, and how they are evaluated.

Targeting **Hard-to-Reach Populations:** Create family-school climate-building activities which invite parents who have been reluctant and/or confused about connecting with the school to participate in events which substantially alter the way they and the school view each other. For example, in one school, teachers, administrators, and parents expressed a desire to increase the participation of English as Second Language families. Building on the work of a multi-lingual, multi-cultural parent committee already involved in outreach, a cross-cultural forum was planned. At the forum, conducted in several major languages (Spanish, Urdu, Chinese, Russian), parents were asked to talk about what school was like in their countries of origin and how it differed from their children's current school experience. The teachers had the opportunity to learn more about the different school systems and cultures that immigrant children have experienced, and the families learned more about the American school system and expectations for parent involvement. This experience became a starting point for demonstrating the school's interest in and respect for the parents. Ideas were generated for easing comfort and overcoming language barriers for these parents. Parents offered to help the school in varying capacities. Children were involved in helping design the invitations to their parents and decorating the reception room where snacks from different countries were served.

Targeting **Students at Risk for Being Held Back: "Holdover" Meetings:** These are multi-family problem-solving meetings with school administrators and teachers which address the problems threatening the educational progress of groups of students at risk for being held back in their grade level. Students and parents are encouraged to identify the children's strengths and areas needing improvement. The focus is on finding solutions as opposed to threat about non-promotion. The concerns raised in the group meetings become the focus of individual planning sessions for parents of each student with the teacher. The school uses the activity to communicate that when students have learning difficulties the staff is concerned and wants to work actively with the students and their parents/families to solve the problems.

Targeting **Students Transitioning from Elementary to Junior High School or Middle School:** Meetings with 5th or 6th grade students, their families and school staff are held to help students prepare for the move to secondary school (for the 6th or 7th grade). At these meetings, fears and hopes are discussed, and constructive guidelines to help students and their parents through the social and academic transition are identified. If possible, administrators, students and/or teachers from the junior high school are present to answer questions and offer suggestions about what is helpful. Activities focusing on this articulation to the next level are also held at the secondary level. Parents and students engage in interactive learning activities in various subject areas. These experiences showcase the nature of the learning experience and expectations at the next level. Families tour the new school and have opportunities to talk informally with administrators and teachers. Special programs may be featured.

Targeting **Multicultural Communities:** Activities that simultaneously celebrate the many cultures in a school strengthen families' links to the school and enrich students' curricular experience. Children can engage their families in discussions about their culture of origin through interviews that they devise and write in class. Information gleaned from interviews becomes the basis for murals, songs, plays and stories created in classroom by the students and those family members who can attend. School-wide events, including sharing of ethnic food, dances, and plays, extend the numbers of families and children involved. The emphasis is on activities that involve parents, staff, and students in meaningful learning experiences together. Opportunities for families to interact with each other as members of the same school community build a climate of connections on behalf of all children's learning growth.

Targeting **Test-Takers:** Some schools have organized classroom discussion forums for teachers, students and families about how to succeed in learning and in test taking. Testing is the focus of anxiety in many schools. Some schools talk with children and parents about how to manage anxiety about "test-taking." They join that with a focus on how to increase interest in reading. At one school, a year-long project about reading evolved from initial workshops about feeling more confident about testing. Parents with the time worked as reading volunteers in the school; parents who were unable to work at the school offered suggestions for involving their children in reading at home. Reading thus became a family-school-community endeavor at the same time that anxiety about tests was reduced.

Additional Examples of Elective Climate-building Activities including School Staff, Students and Parents/Families:

- Family-School Yard Committee Formation
- Orientation to First Grade
- Family Reading Night
- Family Math Night
- English as a Second Language (ESL) Breakfast
- Collaborative Family-School Drug Prevention Program
- Fifth Grade Articulation to Middle School
- Family-School Career Day Fashion Show
- Family-School Asthma Workshop
- Family-School Forum (discussion forum) for Adolescents, Parents and Staff

SESSION 20
Handout 3

Multiple Perspectives Form

School Staff

_____
_____
_____
_____
_____
_____
_____

Parents

_____
_____
_____
_____
_____
_____
_____

Children

_____
_____
_____
_____
_____
_____
_____

End of Session 20

SESSION 21: How do we implement a successful elective climate-building activity?

Rationale:

The experience of planning an elective climate-building activity will deepen school personnel's awareness of how routine events can become more collaborative and how to plan and implement problem-focused climate-building activities. As they design a specific event, they will increase their skill in matching activities to the issue at hand; better understand how to prepare themselves, the student and their parents for such an activity; and gain knowledge of how to evaluate an elective climate-building event.

Goals

- To develop a plan to implement a successful, elective climate-building activity.
- To increase skills at assessing the success of the activity.

Handouts/Materials

- *Multiple Family Problem-Solving Form*
- *Activity Planning Form*
- *Implementation Form*
- *Kindergarten Orientation Feedback Form*
- *Summary of Results from Kindergarten Orientation Feedback*

Introduction

Say: **Today we are going to continue planning elective climate-building activities. Last time we began to consider which issues you wanted to address in your schools. Now we will actually plan climate-building activities around these issues.**

Activity I. Activity Planning

INSTRUCTIONS

1. Break the participants into school-based small groups.

2. Review the handout that the participants began completing in the previous session *(Multiple Perspectives Form)* or distribute a blank copy.

3. Say: **Please complete both the Activity Planning Form and the Implementation Form no matter what your elective activity is. This will help you to think through and organize an action plan for your activity including specific tasks, dates, and responsibilities.**

   I'm also going to distribute the Multiple Families Problem-Solving Form in case the event you've decided to focus on in your school targets an issue that relates to a specific constituency.

4. Distribute *Multiple Families Problem-Solving Form, Activity Planning Form* and *Implementation Form* Handouts #1, #2 and #3. Ask participants to generate a plan based on ideas and messages that they brainstormed in previous session.

Activity II. Feedback Mechanism

INSTRUCTIONS

1. Say: **Develop a feedback mechanism so you can assess the effectiveness of this activity. This can be a simple questionnaire to be filled out by people as they leave and/or a follow-up meeting to discuss the event. I'll distribute examples of a kindergarten orientation feedback form and its results.**

2. Distribute *Summary of Results from Kindergarten Orientation Feedback* Handout #5 and *Sample Data Pages for Analysis* Handout #6

Activity III. Sharing Plans/Reflection

INSTRUCTIONS

1. Reporting out:

Ask a representative from each group to present the group's plan. Invite other group members to make suggestions in a constructive manner. Develop with the whole group a set of guidelines for implementation, which can help each school create a successful climate-building activity.

SESSION 21
Handout 1

Multiple Family Problem-Solving Form

Meeting Flow Steps

1. Overview

2. Finding Facts

3. Blocking Blame

4. Checking for Consensus

5. Determining a Decision

6. Arriving at Action

Steps for Collaborative Planning/Problem Solving

1. Define Concerns- *e.g., low reading scores, physical aggression, racial tensions*

_____

_____

2. Set Priority- *identify one issue to work on*

_____

_____

3. Determine Target- *e.g., entire school, incoming Kindergarten class, ESL program*

_____

_____

4. Identify Constituencies within the Target – *e.g., teachers, parents, students, other family members, support staff, administration, community, office staff, kitchen staff, custodial staff, community agencies.*

_____

_____

5. Select Goal - *e.g., to increase reading scores, to develop new norms in the school around fighting, to get to know one another, to develop pride in school to establish a school-wide homework policy.*

_____

_____

6. Plan Activity- *include the following:*

    a.   Pre-activity Events - *e.g., invitations, publicity.*

_____

_____

    b.   Activity or Series of Activities - *include steps to implement the activity and to evaluate the success of the event as information for future planning.*

_____

_____

_____

_____

    c.   Post-activity Events - *e.g., disseminating information about the event to others, following up on decisions made, developing subsequent activities in a series.*

_____

_____

_____

SESSION 21
Handout 2

Activity Planning Form

INSTRUCTIONS: Use the following elements of school climate as a checklist to plan an activity to fulfill a significant educational goal or deal with a major issue of concern at your school.

Issue or Concern:

_____

Activity:

_____

ELEMENTS OF CLIMATE:

Messages to be conveyed (values, norms, beliefs):

_____

_____

_____

Individual and/or groups who should be involved:

_____

_____

_____

Collaborative interactions necessary to reach goal and convey message:

_____

_____

_____

Physical characteristics and materials that convey the message:

_____

_____

SESSION 21
Handout 3

Implementation Form

1. Time and Date:

_____

2. Place:

_____

3. Invitations:

_____

4. Security:

_____

5. Sign-in:

_____

6. Refreshments:

_____

7. Set Up:

_____

8. Purchasing, Receipts, Reimbursements:

_____

9. Clean up:

_____

10. Assessment/Feedback:

_____

11. Follow-up:

_____

SESSION 21
Handout 4

Activity Feedback Form

Name (optional): _____   Child's Classroom: _____

Date of Activity: _____

1. What did you like most about today's events?

_____

_____

2. How different was this activity from events that you have attended before at schools? (Circle one)

| 1 | 2 | 3 | 4 | 5 | 6 | 7 |

Not at all different   Extremely different

How was it different?

_____

_____

3. How helpful was this in learning about your child's life at school? (Circle one)

| 1 | 2 | 3 | 4 | 5 | 6 | 7 |

Not at all helpful   Extremely helpful

Check all the items that were helpful:

_____ I got to know the teacher better.

_____ The teacher got to know me better.

_____ I was able to see my child in the classroom.

_____ I was able to see my child's work in the classroom.

_____ My child was excited that I came to school.

_____ I got to see the other children my child goes to school with.

_____ I was able to meet some of the other parents in the classroom.

_____ I showed my child that I cared about him/her.

_____ I got ideas for helping my child.

_____ Other _____

4. What would you like to see done at future events where students, parents, and teacher meet together?

_____

_____

Other comments:

_____

_____

SESSION 21
Handout 5

Sample: Summary of Results from Kindergarten Orientation Feedback
Family-School Partnership Program
Summary of Results from Kindergarten Orientation Feedback

Overview: On the bus back from the PS 152 Kindergarten Celebrations, we distributed the attached questionnaire to the parents. Twenty-three parents filled out the questionnaire and returned it to us. This is a summary of the ratings and comments that they provided to us.

1. What did you like most about today's events?

32% said that they liked being in school with their child.

26% said it was a positive, joyous event.

21% said it was having parents, students and teacher all together.

11 % said it was that their child felt good about the event.

2. How different was this to events that you have attended before at school?

33% said it was the first school event they had attended.

20% said it was the food.

13% said that it was a happy and joyous event.

13% said it was being with the students and teacher at the same time.

3. What would you like to see done at future events where students, parents, and teacher meet together? Other comments:

38% said more of the same.

31% said to have parents participate more and/or have more sharing.

23% said to spend more time together.

23% said to have enough bus transportation for everyone.

13% said to make sure that children whose parents didn't come could eat and participate with the other children and parents.

SESSION 21

Handout 6

Sample Data Pages for Analysis
Elementary School Kindergarten Celebration, Nov. 21, 1991

N = 23 (Out of total of 125)

1. What did you like most about today's events?

2. How different was this to events that you have attended before at schools? (Circle one) X= 4.

| 1 | 2 | 3 | 4 | 5 | 6 | 7 |

Not at all different   Extremely different

    How was it different?

3. How helpful was this in learning about your child's life at school? (Circle one) X = 6.05

| 1 | 2 | 3 | 4 | 5 | 6 | 7 |

Not at all different   Extremely different

    Check all the items that were helpful:

    N = 23 responses

    <u>21</u> I got to know the teacher better.

    <u>19</u> The teacher got to know me better.

    <u>22</u> I was able to see my child in the classroom.

    <u>17</u> I was able to see my child's work in the classroom.

    <u>20</u> My child was excited that I came to school.

    <u>21</u> I got to see the other children my child goes to school with

    <u>21</u> I was able to meet some of the other parents in the classroom.

    <u>23</u> I showed my child that I cared about him/her.

    Other _____

4. What would you like to see done at future events where students, parents, and teachers meet together?

5. Other comments? (Please use back)

End of Session 21

SESSION 22: How can we collaborate with families at home?

Rationale:

So far we've discussed collaborative activities built on the presumption of the family's presence in the school. Whether families can come to school or not, there are meaningful ways to involve them in their children's education. In this session we explore ways to collaboratively link the family and the school through various at-home activities.

Goals

- To understand the range of possible at-home collaborative activities.
- To explore ways to involve students in structuring reflective conversations with their parents.
- To create an at-home family-school activity.

Handouts/Materials

- *Types of Collaborative At-Home Activities*
- *Family Discussion of Mr. Mercier's Unity Day Song*
- *Work-Play Family Homework*
- *Parent Homework Interview*
- *The Sharing Portfolio Project*
- *Letter to Parents*
- White board/Smart Board or chart paper

Introduction

Say: **So far, we've discussed family-school collaboration as an endeavor that takes place at school with family, teacher, and child present. Yet, as many of you well know and in fact may have thought throughout our previous sessions, it's often difficult or even impossible for some families to get to school. School events may conflict with work or training programs in which families are enrolled. Parents may have young children or elderly relatives who can't be left alone or in school-provided childcare. Additionally, some parents are reluctant to come to school until they feel certain that neither they nor their child will be blamed or put on the spot.**

Whether families come to school or not, there are meaningful ways to involve them in their child's education. In this session we will explore ways to create at-home collaboration, which connect families to their child and the school.

Though these activities are not intended to draw families into the school, they may have the unintended benefit of encouraging reluctant parents to venture into the school once they've had positive and worthwhile experiences with their child at home.

Activity I. Reflection

INSTRUCTIONS

1. *Think about it.* Ask participants to reflect on the following:

   - *Have any of you tried at-home collaborative activities?*

   - *What has worked, and what hasn't?*

2. As participants cite activities, list them on chart paper.

With one color marker, indicate which activities worked and with another, those that did not work.

3. Once the list is complete, ask participants to look for patterns in what worked and what didn't, and list those themes on a separate sheet. Review the elements and ask what's gotten in the way.

4. Say: **What concerns you about what's happened previously and what might happen this time?**

5. Generate a list of concerns with the participants. Some examples might be:

   - Parents get too critical of the child
   - Parents don't help

6. Ask: **What are some ways of addressing these concerns?**

Share the list below with participants and ask them if there are additional items they'd like to add:

Some Possible Solutions:

> - Kids get excited about a specific project and, acting as ambassadors, urge families to do it with them.
> - It is a meaningful exercise for both family member and child and therefore encourages all to get involved.
> - The person doing the exercise with the child does not have to be a parent. It could be a grandparent, older sibling, aunt, etc.
> - Introducing the exercise with a letter from the teacher to the adults in the household first could articulate its purpose, offer suggestions about when and how to structure it, and explain guidelines for interactions among family members. This highlights the activity's value and makes it safe.

7. Once you have reviewed the list, say: **We will add to the list as we review examples of at-home collaborative activities today.**

Activity II. Four Types of Activities

INSTRUCTIONS

1. Say: **We are going to take a look at four types of at-home activities.**

2. Distribute Handouts #2-6 as a packet. Ask participants to look at *Mr. Mercier's Unity Day* exercise.

Type 1: Extending Traditional School Activities to Home (Unity Day)

3. Say: **This first example, Mr. Mercier's Unity Day activity, represents a way to move beyond families as audience by involving them in children's preparation for a performance. This exercise was created by a teacher in a bilingual Haitian Creole program whose class was going to perform a song he had written for a Unity Day assembly in his school. He asked families to discuss the song's meaning and then help children memorize the words.**

4. *Think about it.* Please look the activity over and think about the following:

- *What are your reactions to this exercise?*

- *How well does it address your concerns and/or incorporate our list of solutions about at-home activities?*

- *Is there anything in this approach we could add to our list?*

Type 2: Activity At Home to Bring Back To School (Work/Play)

5. Say: **This next handout is an example of family homework- a series of activities related to children's experiences at school. This was created by the administrators**

and teachers at a school where parents of young elementary students were concerned about the absence of traditional worksheets and confused by what appeared to be too much "playtime." After an on-site hands-on workshop about the link between playing and learning, the school sent these materials home along with an explanation of the learn/play connection for families who couldn't attend. They wanted to encourage parents to engage their children in play that had educational and emotional benefits.

6. *Think about it.* Invite participants to look this over and think about the following:

- *What do you notice in these materials?*

- *How well do they address the concerns you raised about family cooperation in doing at home activities?*

- *Is there anything we could add to our list from this activity?*

Type 3: Having Students Generate Structured Ways to Talk With Parents (Homework Interview, Sharing Portfolio Project)

7. Say: **These two examples represent teachers' efforts to engage students in actively creating the framework/questions for a positive conversation with their families about their schoolwork. In both, the teacher worked with students to generate a list of questions that they would ask parents and in the case of the older children a list that the parents would ask them. Students acted as researchers collecting information from parents or family members that they then pooled, collated and discussed with their classmates.**

The first example is from another Haitian Creole bilingual class. The teacher had noticed that parents seemed confused about what role they should play in relation to their children's homework. She suspected that because expectations of parents and the approach to many subject areas, especially math, in the US and Haiti were so different, families did not know whether or how to help their children. Together she and the students generated this list of questions about homework. Then the children collectively analyzed the results.

Based on these 'findings' the teacher invited families to a homework workshop where they discussed their questions and identified ways to help students. One way was having designated homework helpers – e.g., parents who understood the American approach to math – in the areas where the majority of children lived who would be available to help students in the class.

The second example is the work of a middle school teacher whose students had developed art portfolios. He wanted to be sure that that they were able to share and discuss their work with families in ways that were meaningful, supportive and productive.

He organized this process into a five stage exercise:

- *First,* he sent a letter home explaining the exercise and including a list of guidelines developed by the students in their own words.
- *Next,* he helped the students develop two series of questions about the portfolios - one for a family member to ask children and the other for children to ask a family member.
- *Then*, the family member and the students met and talked at home.
- *After* the at-home meeting, the class met to share their experiences and compare responses to the questions. At this meeting they also brainstormed and then honed a series of follow-up questions to ask their families about the experience.
Finally, approximately two weeks after the classroom meeting, students interviewed their parents and then shared and analyzed the interview data they had collected.

8. *Think about it.* Please take a few moments to look over these two examples and reflect on the following:

- *What are your reactions?*
- *How might they address the concerns or add to the solutions about at-home collaboration?*

Type 4: Helping Family Members Find Ways to Initiate Conversations at Home (Questions from 2nd grade class)

9. Say: **This final example is the work of second grade teacher who had heard many parents complain that their children didn't talk to them about their school day. She knew that they were eager to hear more than "It was ok," and decided that a letter outlining the parts of the day and possible questions for each might be helpful.**

10. *Think about it.* Please look it over and reflect:

- *What do you think of her effort?*
- *How helpful would it be in addressing your concerns about collaborative conversations at home?*
- *Does it add to our solutions?*

Activity III. Reflection on Activities

INSTRUCTIONS

1. **Say: Now that we've reviewed these examples of four types of at-home collaboration, I'd like to give you the opportunity to expand on what we've seen.**

   Right now, I'd like you to turn to a partner and pick the 1st, 2nd or final example. Then, together, please brainstorm ways that you as teachers could make these even more collaborative and more likely to happen at home.

   Give participants about 5 minutes for this exercise.

2. Say: **Please share your ideas. Let's go example by example. Who chose example 1, Mr. Mercier's letter? How might it have become more collaborative?**

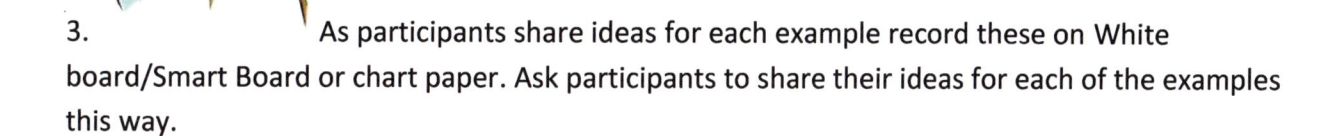

3. As participants share ideas for each example record these on White board/Smart Board or chart paper. Ask participants to share their ideas for each of the examples this way.

4. When they have finished sharing, Say: **Let's look these over: what do you notice in the ideas you've come up with? What are some of the themes?**

Possible examples:

> - Students play a more active role in generating questions and laying the guidelines for the work.
> - There are follow-up conversations for the activities where student and family member discuss what it was like for them to talk or play in this way.
> - Teachers talk the activity up to students so they are enthusiastic about it and urge family members to engage with them.

> - Teachers write an explanatory letter to families about the educational and emotional value of these activities.
> - Teachers emphasize the educational and social importance of processing these at-home activities in school. S/he explains that the students will share their experiences with the class and the conversations will become the basis for further activity in school and at home.

Let's go back to our list of concerns and possible solutions one last time. How would the ideas you've generated help to address the concerns and add to the solutions?

Activity IV. Modifying One Activity

INSTRUCTIONS

1. Say: **Now each of you, either singly, in pairs, or in small groups, will have the opportunity to design an at-home collaborative activity for your classroom.**

2. Distribute *Types of Collaborative Activities* Handout #1.

3. Say: **Please look over the examples we've discussed and choose one you would like to adapt to your classroom. Alternatively, you can choose an activity from the "Other Ideas" section at the bottom of the handout.**

   As you work, please be sure to check to see that you've incorporated some of the items on solutions list we've generated and the ways we've identified to heighten collaboration into your plan.

Give participants 15 minutes to plan.

4. *Think about it.* Now I'd like you to share your ideas with the group and reflect on the following:

   - *As you modified the activity for your classroom, what challenges emerged?*

   - *How do-able does this now seem to you?*

   - *What could make it more likely that you will be able to actually do it with your class?*

SESSION 22
Handout 1

Types of Collaborative At-Home Activities

1. Extending Traditional School Activities to Home:
- *Family Discussion of Mr. Mercier's Unity Day Song:* This is an example of the way one teacher turned a typical parent as audience situation into a more collaborative and connected experience for families. Prior to the event he distributed this letter providing a format for parents' and children's discussion of the topic – unity – about which they would be performing. After the play he invited those parents who were able to attend back to the classroom for further discussion.

2. Activity At Home to Bring Back To School:
- *Work-Play Family Homework:* This is an example of homework developed by K-2 teachers interested in helping families understand more about the link between work and play. Once the assignments have been completed and turned in, the teachers will compile them into a book, which all students will take home and share with their families.

3. Having Students Generate Structured Ways To Talk With Parents:
- *Parent Homework Interview*: This was distributed by a teacher in a bilingual class. Many of her students' parents were having difficulty helping their children with homework because of language problems and/or differences in the way subjects such as math are taught in their countries of origin. She decided to conduct a "Homework Helping Workshop" in class but first had students interview their parents about homework. Prior to the interview – which students helped generate – she prepared them by role-playing in class and discussing how and when to approach their parents with the interview. Once the interviews were completed, students and the teacher analyzed them; counting how many parents gave specific responses and discussing differences in their own and their parents' homework experiences. Even those children whose parents could not attend the workshop got to represent their parents there.
- *The Sharing Portfolio Project:* This is the work of a middle school teacher whose students had developed art portfolios. He wanted to ensure that that they were able to share and discuss their work with families in ways that were meaningful, supportive and productive. With students' input, he structured at-home conversations about the work that allowed for constructive reflection between students and their families.

4. Helping Family Members Find Ways to Initiate Conversations at Home:

- *Letter to Parents:* Developed by a 2nd grade teacher, this letter was intended to help parents find ways to initiate conversation with their children about their school day in meaningful ways.

Other Ideas:

- *Collaborative Newsletters:* A school could develop a collaborative family-school newsletter. Parents and children could jointly write articles together about school events and present interviews they conduct with families and teachers. Parents might send their questions about school to a "Dear Students" column in which students provide answers.
- *Pre-Holiday Interviews:* Together with their students, many teachers develop interviews for families about specific holidays or events such as Christmas, summer vacation, birthdays, etc., which explore how they were celebrated when they were children, what they like best about them, etc. Students then share the results as a class and often invite their parents to join them in a discussion of the results and a celebration.
- *Family History/When You Were Young Interviews:* These entail designing interviews with the students that they conduct with their families. They can be the basis for family-school events, class discussions and projects. One teacher had his 4th grade students interview their parents about their lives "then and now." They then used the results as the basis for murals they designed (inviting available parents to join them) as the scenery for a school play about history.
- *Family Reading Journal:* This can either be a journal maintained by each child and his/her family about books they read together or a class journal that circulates from home to home. For a class journal, each family reads a book and then writes about it (or answers specific questions about it) and returns the journal to school. The teacher then sends it along to another family. By the end of the year each family has not only contributed but also had the opportunity to read others' comments about books.
- *Family Reading Activities:* This curriculum can be the basis for parent/child homework assignments that are non-threatening, quick and fun.

SESSION 22
Handout 2

Family Discussion of Mr. Mercier's Unity Day Song

Dear Parents and Guardians,

Our class is busy preparing a skit for the Unity Assembly, May 24th and 26th. We are very excited about the skit and the Unity Day theme – that working together we can accomplish more than we can alone.

In fact, I have written new words to the traditional Haitian song _____ and would like to share that here with you so that you can discuss it with your child.

Here are some ideas for helping your child learn the song and discussing its theme with him or her.

Please read the song with your child. Invite him/her to sing it to you and make sure s/he knows it by heart.

Please read these questions with your child. Be sure each of you gives your own answers and then compare/discuss them with each other.

1) Pick one or two words in this song that make you think about unity. Why do they make you think of unity?

2) Can you think of something you tried to do alone which you learned you could only do with someone else's help? What was it? How was it different when someone else helped you?

What people do each of you need in your lives? Children, what would happen if you didn't have the teacher, the bus driver, the school custodian or even your parents in your lives?

SESSION 22
Handout 3

Work-Play Family Homework

<u>Learning through Play – Playing to Learn</u>

Hands-on Activities

1. Newspaper balls and bat (see attached)

2. Play-dough (see attached)

3. Salt-dough (see attached)

4. Magazine and newspaper collage: Using old newspapers and magazines, have your child create their own works of art by cutting and pasting different images.

5. Garbage play: Collect old cereal, tissues, and macaroni boxes to be stuffed and used for building homemade blocks.

Verbal Interactive Games

1. Pretend: Your child might like to role play different situations and characters in the world (house, school, store, etc)

2. "I spy…" first person sees something and the second person has to try to guess what they see (or spy).

3. "I see _____, what do you see?" First person says, "I see." Second person or group says, "What do you see?" First person says: "I see everybody (choose activity)" – rubbing head, tapping belly, etc, and the second person/group does it.

4. 20 Questions: First person has an image in their head and the second person needs to guess what it is asking only questions that have yes/no answers.

5. "I'm thinking of a number…" first person has a number in their head from 1-10 and the second person must try to guess it using clues.

Hands-On Activities Materials and Directions

- Newspaper balls and bat:

    Balls: Take 2 pages of newspaper and crunch it up into a ball. Put tape around the ball to play catch, etc.

    Bat: 4-5 pieces of paper rolled up and taped to make a bat.

- Salt dough:

    Ingredients:
    3 cups of all-purpose flour
    1 cup of salt
    1 ¼ cup of warm water

    Directions:
    Mix the flour and the salt together and slowly add the warm water. If you would like your sculpture to last you could bake in an oven for 45 minutes at 250 degrees. Unbaked, this mixture will last for one week in the refrigerator.

- Playdough:

    Ingredients:
    2 cups of water
    2 cups of flour
    1 cup of salt
    2 tablespoons of oil
    4 teaspoons of cream of tartar
    Add food coloring as needed

    Directions:
    Mix ingredients together. Keep the playdough covered to help it last longer. If it hardens it must be thrown away.

Reflection

1. Which family homework assignment did you try?

2. Who did you play with?

3. Where did you play?

4. When did you play?

5. Was it fun? Why was it fun?

6. What was the best or worst part?

7. Do you play any other kinds of games with your family?

SESSION 22
Handout 4

Parent Homework Interview

Dear Class:

This is a good time of the year to talk with your parents about homework. The questions on this sheet will help you talk with your parents and will help me learn more about their ideas. Here are directions for asking the questions and doing an interview:

- It is very important that you try to write down exactly what your parents say when they answer a question.
- It is fine to ask a grown-up to talk slowly or to stop talking for a minute while you record what they have said.
- It is also important to write only what the grown-up says, not what you think or would like them to say.
- When they have finished answering one part to the question and you have finished writing, ask the next question.

1. How did you do your homework when you were my age? Where did you do it? Did anybody help you? Who?
_____
_____
_____

2. Now let's talk about my homework. What are the subjects you feel confident helping me with?_____
_____
_____

3. What subjects are difficult for you to help me with? Why?
_____
_____
_____

4. What do you think Mrs. Dominique expects you to help me with in school?
_____
_____
_____

SESSION 22
Handout 5

The Sharing Portfolio Project

Dear Families,

As you may recall, your child has been participating in a special project with a small group of students who are compiling portfolios of their work that they will share with you. They will bring home their portfolios in late May and early June. They hope to show them to you to review and discuss them with you.

Could you please spend 30 minutes (or as much time as you need) looking over the work with your child? The students have developed two sets of specific questions. One set is questions for you to ask them about their efforts. These should be the focus of your conversation with them. <u>We ask that you stick to the written questions only.</u>

The second set is questions your children would also like to ask you about their work. In planning their conversations with you, the students have come up with a few suggestions about how to make this a positive experience that you will both want to repeat. Here, in their own words, are their suggestions:

- Please set aside a quiet time (not while you are cooking or doing the dishes) to talk with your child.
- Please sit down next to your child and give her/him your full attention.
- Take the time to talk about this and not anything else.
- Please do not change the subject. Pay attention to what s/he is showing you.
- Please say positive things. Look for the good stuff, not the bad stuff.
- Remember: No one is perfect.
- Try to appreciate the work that is done and not focus on what is missing.

The students are very excited about sharing their work with you. We hope you both enjoy the experience.

Thank you!

Questions for Family Members to ask Kids:

- What did you learn when you were doing this project?
- Did you have fun?
- What was this project about?
- Did you work hard on it?
- Were you interested in it?
- What was most difficult about making this project?

Questions for Kids to ask Family Members:

- Did you like my work?
- Do you think I could improve in this work?
- What can I do to make it better?
- What's most interesting to you about it?
- Does any of this work make you proud of me?
- Do you think I did my best?
- What do you feel when you see my pictures?
- Which one do you like best/prefer?

SESSION 22
Handout 6

Letter to Parents

Dear Parents:

Some children come home and give you a full account of their day (and possibly everyone else's!) while others never mention school and when asked about it directly say "I forget" or "Nothing." Children of the second type may seem to be less involved in school, yet it may actually be the opposite. They may become so immersed in each part of their day that everything that has happened before disappears from their thoughts.

I have found that it is sometimes helpful to ask more specific questions calling times of the day by the names we use in the classroom, naming possible activities they might have done etc. To help you do this, here are some of the particular labels we use, and some questions you might ask:

Meeting	Morning Choices	Art
Sharing	Activity Time	Library
Group lesson	Quiet reading	Music
Calendar	Math games	Problem-solving
Handwriting	Class journal	Story Time
Writing time	Reading	Gym

Here are some possible questions:

<u>Meeting</u>: Who was absent today? How many children were absent? Who did the calendar? Who delivered the attendance book to the nurse? What is your helping hand job this week? How many children got pizza today? Do you remember today's date? Do you remember what day of the week it is?

<u>Sharing</u>: Did anyone share something from home today? Did you share something you did in school? Did anyone else share something he/she did in school?

<u>Handwriting</u>: Did you practice writing any letters today? What were they?

Writing Time: What are you writing about? Did you draw any pictures? Did you put any words to it? Do you have any ideas for a new story? Have you written a book? Did anyone share his or her story/book with the class? What was it about?

Class Journal: What did the class write about today? (Not every day) Did you help with any of the story?

Reading/Quiet Reading Time: What book(s) did you read or look at? Did a friend read to you? Did you share a book with a friend? Did you have a reading conference with Mrs. Schwartz?

Group Lesson: Did you talk about a painting today? An artist? What did you see? What did you discuss? Did you learn a new game? Are you working on a graph?

Problem Solving: What was the math problem you tried to solve today? Were there many ways children used to solve it? Did you think of a way?

Morning Choices or Activity Time: What did you choose? Who did you work with? What were you making? (Choices include: Blocks, balance scales, science table, painting, junk sculptures, drawing, workbench, sewing, sand/water table, card games, geoboards, polydrons, pattern blocks, listening area, reading, writing folders etc!)

Storytime: What book did you listen to today? What was it about?

Naturally, these questions shouldn't turn into a cross-examination, but hopefully they'll spark a dialogue. Good luck!

-Ms. Schwartz☺

End of Session 22

SESSION 23: How can we develop elective collaborative activities with high school populations?

Rationale:

High school parents' options for partnerships with their child's school are less obvious and less numerous than those of elementary school parents. In the elementary setting parents get to know only one classroom teacher each year and are able to form a trusting relationship with her/him. In addition, parents are routinely involved both physically and intellectually in their child's education. For example, they may transport young children to school, sign their homework, help them with schoolwork, or volunteer in the classroom. Parents are usually informed about their child's day-to-day schedule and are fully expected to meet with school personnel -- usually without the child -- if there is a problem.

By contrast, high school parents are much less of a presence in their child's on-going school life. They may not even know the names of all of their child's teachers, and may have very little opportunity to interact with them. Even the most attentive parents may only appear at the school a few times a year -- for report card conferences, back to school night, school performances and athletic events. When there is a problem, parents are not necessarily called into the school. School officials speak to the student. Then they notify the parents and expect them to discipline the student on their own.

These differences in parental involvement are understandably based on the differing maturity levels, developmental needs and life tasks of young children and adolescents. They also reflect typical declining expectations for parental involvement from elementary to secondary grades. Genuine partnerships between schools and families must be forged in ways that are age-appropriate. While elementary school collaboration highlights bringing the child into the discussion as an active participant, high school collaboration entails finding viable roles for the parents that support students but do not undermine their autonomy.

This session will present one elective family-high school climate-building activity. Special attention has been paid to the ways in which high-school students can help conceptualize and organize such events so they feel empowered rather than infantilized.

Goals

- To identify the differences between elementary and high school family-school collaboration.
- To address the challenges of family involvement with adolescents.
- To assess one high school's approach to family-school problem-solving.

Handouts/Materials

- *Activity Planning Form: High School Meeting*
- *Implementation Form: High School Meeting*
- *Collaborative Planning Questions: High School Meeting*
- White board/Smart Board or chart paper

Introduction

Say: **In this session we will discuss ways to apply family-school collaboration to the high school setting. While some of the fundamental concepts remain the same, the approach needs to shift to accommodate the developmental needs, educational experiences, and expectations of high school students and their families.**

Activity I. High School-Specific Context

INSTRUCTIONS

1. Say: **Before we actually describe a high school activity, it may be helpful to contrast the secondary school context with that of the elementary school in terms of the roles and expectations of students and their families.**

2. Divide participants into four small groups. Assign each group one of the four following issues to discuss. If the group is too large for a small group discussion, suggest that each person get with a partner to discuss the issue and then share with the small group.

- The ways in which high schools involve parents.
- Typical ways in which high schools deal with students and families when there is a problem.
- Developmental needs of high school students in relation to their parents' involvement in their school lives.
- How the structure of the school (i.e. scheduling, number of teachers, number of students) affects the roles parents can play.

3. Have the groups list their responses on separate sheets of chart paper as they discuss their topic. Lead a discussion of the issues for high school climate-building activities, and wherever possible contrast these with the elementary school issues. Have participants review each other's lists, ask questions, and make comments or additions. The lists might include the following items:

The ways in which high schools involve parents:
- Parents are involved as audience for recreational and cultural activities.
- Parents are invited to Open School and Meet the Teacher nights.
- Few, if any, informal visits to the school to consult teachers or pick up children take place.
- Little informal school-based contact exists with other parents or with teachers.

Typical ways that high schools deal with students and families when there is a problem:
- Administrators and teachers generally go directly to the student.
- Parents may be informed by mail of chronic or minor problems.
- Parents are consulted in person or by phone only after the problem is considered severe.
- Consultation with parents usually implies the need for disciplinary intervention at home rather than cooperation with the school in solving the problem.
- Contacting the parents implies that the student has 'failed' to handle the problem appropriately on his/her own.

Developmental needs of high school students in relation to their parents' involvement in their school lives:
- Students need to experience autonomy in their school life and in responsibility for completing school-related tasks and activities.
- Students need to experience adults as having a sense of respect for their privacy, i.e. that there are some areas of their lives that are confidential.
- Students need to feel that they are succeeding (or failing) because of their own efforts, not those of their parents, but also feel they are supported and encouraged to do their best.
- Students need to feel empowered to solve problems alone and to learn to accept the help of family members without feeling infantilized.
- Students need to learn to differentiate being a good student from being the obedient child and to value successful experiences as a reflection of their own efforts (with the support of others).
- Students need to develop and maintain their relationships with peers and to experience the approval and acceptance of their peers.

How the structure of the high school affects the roles parents can play:
- Teachers have many more students than elementary school teachers and therefore do not know any one child as well.
- Students have many classes per day and therefore have more than one teacher to deal with.
- Logistically, teachers have difficulty finding the time to make phone calls and schedule meetings with parents.
- Teachers fear that involvement of parents on a regular basis could add even more stress to their already overburdened school lives.

4. Say: **Let's discuss some of the key implications that emerge from these lists in terms of the challenges of working with families in high school settings as distinct from elementary school settings:**

5. List the challenges on chart paper as you lead the discussion. 6.

Possible challenges:
- To create a three-way conversation by bringing the parent (as opposed to the student in the elementary school setting) into the discussion.
- To position students so that they can accept their parents' participation as a reflection of their new status as adolescent and not as an attempt to infantilize them or treat them as inadequate.
- To find a viable role for parents which supports, but does not undermine students' autonomy.
- To define a way for parents to play a collaborative and authoritative vs. a 'big guns' (authoritarian) disciplinary role.
- To redefine the meaning of being a good student from being obedient to adults to succeeding for the sake of one's own future goals and satisfaction.
- To present family-school collaboration to teachers and administrators as a strategy which can be adapted to their taxing scheduling demands and student case loads.
- To convey to students and their families the message that, despite its size and bureaucratic structure, the school cares about each student and wants to work together with them to ensure his/her success.

Say: **To illustrate the way in which an elective activity can be geared to a high school population we will 'walk' through the planning phases of a multi-family problem-focused meeting that was implemented at one high school.**

The school is a large suburban high school with a predominantly white upper middle through lower middle class population. A small group (15) of teachers, administrators and pupil support personnel identified an issue of concern that they had been unable to deal with effectively or efficiently. The issue was how to help seniors in danger of not graduating.

Here is an example of the way in which this particular school designed an elective activity that met the specific needs of its secondary school student and family population and of its staff.

Activity II. A Multi-Family Problem-Solving Session for Seniors in Danger of Not Graduating

INSTRUCTIONS

1. Distribute *Activity-Planning Form: High School* Handout #1 to participants and explain that we will follow the group's planning process to illustrate how one district faced the challenge of involving families of high school students.

2. Say: **As we review these forms, think about the challenges we just discussed and ask yourselves if this plan adequate addresses those challenges. If not, what else should they have done?**

3. *Think about it.* After the plan has been reviewed, ask participants to reflect on the following:

    - *What hesitations do you have about this multi-family approach for high school students and their families?*
    - *What do you see as its strengths?*
    - *If you were going to design a family-school activity for seniors at risk of not graduating, what would you do differently and why?*

4. Explain that there are additional planning tools, which might speak to some of their concerns and questions about such a session.

5. Distribute *Collaborative Planning Questions: High School Meeting* and *Implementation Form: High School Meeting* Handouts #2 and #3.

6. Ask participants to look through them and comment on the way the event was planned and organized.

7. Ask participants how they think these additional forms helped to crystallize the planning process and make the event more meaningful and successful.

8. Record responses on the white board/Smart Board or chart paper.

SESSION 23
Handout 1

Activity Planning Form: High School Meeting

INSTRUCTIONS: Use the following elements of school climate as a checklist to plan an activity to fulfill a significant educational goal or deal with a major issue of concern at your school.

Issue or Concern:

How to help seniors in danger of not graduating complete the necessary requirements for graduation by including significant family members and school personnel in the collaborative problem-solving process. Methods of warning, motivating, or providing extra resources for these students have been unsuccessful and inordinately time consuming for teachers and administrators.

Activity:

A preparatory meeting with seniors in danger of not graduating to inform them about the proposed multi-family session. The meeting provides them with the opportunity to react to the idea, involves them in determining the best way to inform parents about the multi-family session and engages them in planning the meeting itself.

A multi-family meeting with these seniors and their families to identify ways in which the students, families, and school personnel could collaborate to increase seniors' possibility of graduating.

ELEMENTS OF CLIMATE:

Message to be conveyed (values, norms beliefs):

To the students:
- We respect your opinions and value your input about how to best help your parents work together with us and with you so you can graduate.
- We understand how difficult it is for you to have your parents involved at this point in your academic career, but their involvement does not mean that you are being treated "like a baby." Rather it means that they can be a resource to you at a time when you need help. Being an adult means knowing when to seek help from others.
- This meeting is not merely being imposed on you. It is not a punishment meeting. We want to have a positive meeting where options for graduation can be explored and planned. We are giving you the opportunity to shape the meeting so it can be most helpful to you.

To the students and their families:
- We care about your children and want to do everything we can to work with them and you to help them graduate. We believe that these students can graduate if they utilize the resources available to them at home, at school, and within themselves.
- We want to hear from you so we can understand your concerns and find the best way(s) to insure your child's graduation. Graduation can still be a realistic goal. "We haven't given up on you." There are numerous things that can get in the way of graduation, but there are also concrete steps one can take to understand what needs to be done and be prepared to do them.

To the parents:
- You do have an appropriate and helpful role to play in helping your child to graduate.
- Your child's current situation does not mean that you have failed as a parent or that your child has failed to establish his/her independence.

Individuals and/or groups who should be involved:

At the preparatory meeting: All seniors in danger of failing a subject that would prevent graduation, school faculty, administrators and pupil support personnel.

At the multi-family meeting: Seniors in danger of not graduating, their parents/guardians or other family members, teacher representatives from each department, administrators and pupil support personnel.

Collaborative interactions necessary to reach goals and convey messages:

At the preparatory meeting with the seniors:
- Opportunity for seniors to express their concerns about a multi-family meeting with their parents.
- A non-punitive exchange between seniors and school staff about the purposes for and possible benefits of the meeting.
- Discussion between seniors and school staff about how best to inform parents about the meeting and how to conduct the meeting to make it most effective and comfortable for them.
- Collaborative composition by seniors and school staff of the letter informing parents about the meeting and planning of the meeting itself.

At the multi-family meeting:
- A discussion among participants about which steps or behaviors are necessary if these seniors were to graduate.
- Sharing of information about what seniors could do even at this late date to reach graduation.

- Private discussions about the situations of specific students with individual faculty members and/or administrators.
- Creation and signing of individual (written) contracts clarifying what each party--student, parents and teachers--must do to ensure the senior's graduation.
- Clarification of channels for follow-up and/or feedback among seniors, families and school staff.

Physical characteristics and materials that convey the message:
- Meetings held in a room large enough so chairs can be arranged in a circle that accommodates a large group.
- All participants including families and school personnel sit in a circle together.
- Refreshments served.
- Families and school personnel are interspersed.

SESSION 23
Handout 2

Implementation Form: High School Meeting

1. Time and Date: Meetings should be held early in the second semester or as soon as it is possible to identify seniors at risk of not graduating. Meetings should be held either early in the morning before school or in the evening to accommodate working parents.

2. Place: Meetings should be held at the school in an open, non-threatening location e.g., not in the administrative offices or in the auditorium where chairs cannot be arranged in a circle.

3. Invitations: Seniors need to be consulted and involved in determining how best to word the parents' invitation to the meeting. The language of the invitation provides the students with a positive frame for the meeting and its objective.

4. Security: A person stationed at a desk at the entry greeting participants and checking that they are in the right place.

5. Sign-in: Sign-in sheets for students and families at the door.

6. Refreshments: Snacks and beverages. Students help plan and purchase beverages, which are available before and after the meeting.

7. Set Up: Students and school staff set up the room.

8. Purchasing, Receipts, Reimbursements: In accordance with school policy.

9. Clean up: Students, volunteer parents and staff members.

10. Assessment/Feedback: Anecdotal information from teachers about seniors (and their parents) who sought them out after the meeting to determine what was required to ensure that they pass the course. School data about the number of at-risk seniors (attending the meeting) who were able to graduate this year as compared with seniors who failed to graduate in previous years. Phone interviews with participating parents and face-to-face interviews with participating seniors. Note: A short evaluation form should also be administered and collected at the end of the meeting.

11. Follow-up: Sharing results of the interviews with relevant school staff. Discussion of how to improve the preparation, meeting and follow-up process for seniors in coming years.

SESSION 23
Handout 3

Collaborative Planning Questions: High School Meeting

1. How to involve central and peripheral staff as active participants in planning and implementation:
Even if a small core group of teachers and administrators function as the primary planners, it is important to inform and get input about the meeting from those teachers who instruct the at-risk seniors. Otherwise, they may feel left out of the process and may be less comfortable about collaborating with at-risk seniors and their families. Who is the first person that you need to talk with about implementing this activity? What are you asking this person to do? What is your goal?

Possible means of informing these teachers include:

- Distribution of a memo or email informing the teachers about the meeting, outlining proposed plans and soliciting their advice.

- Inviting these teachers to attend a planning session and to indicate their level of interest in participating in planning, implementing, conducting or follow up.

- Circulating frequent updates about the planning process and inviting comments and suggestions.

2. How to involve parents in planning and implementation:
After consultation with students about how best to inform and involve their parents, it would be helpful to invite their parents to the meeting and encourage them to submit ideas for topics to be discussed and to suggest how they think the meeting can be most successful.

3. How to involve students in planning and preparation:
As we have noted throughout the completed Activity Planning Form, it is essential to involve high school students in the planning and preparation of the meeting if it is to succeed. Unless they feel that their autonomy and maturity is acknowledged, they are not likely to participate actively or commit themselves to the collaboration process. Students need to feel that they have had some voice and control in the way in which their parents are engaged in the process and the way in which the meeting is organized. They are generally most interested in opportunities in which they can be seen operating in competent ways by their parents. They are most worried about being embarrassed or shamed, and they will participate actively when they trust that these risks are unlikely.

End of Session 23

SESSION 24: How can we reach populations with special needs?

Rationale:

For most students and families, the activities we've described provide a bridge between home and school. This bridge lays the foundation for further productive interactions that encourage students' maximum educational, social, and emotional growth.

However, there are families who, despite the best intentions and motivations, have greater difficulty connecting in positive ways to the school. Often, these families have children or family members whose special needs are so all-consuming that they prevent students from getting to school frequently enough to establish and/or sustain a meaningful bond with school personnel. Special needs range from problems with the emotional, the psychological or the physical aspects of a child's or a family member's daily existence. In many cases these are issues that are shared by several families in a school.

Multi-family meetings with special populations provide a framework for linking families in similar situations to each other and helping them view the school as a place which helps them solve problems rather than as a bureaucratic monolith which lacks compassion for their plight. A collaborative response to specific special needs not only represents an opportunity to normalize families' and children's fears and struggles but also becomes a vehicle for finding common solutions to the obstacles they face.

In this session we will present an overview of one such multi-family-school activity: a series of workshops for asthmatic children and their families in an inner city elementary school. We offer this description as an exemplar of how such climate-building activities were used to address the specific needs of a particular subgroup in a school as well as to contribute to the general school climate by way of demonstrating "how the school does its business."

The session represents a summary of a series of four workshops conducted at this school. The Activity Planning Form is a framework for our presentation of the goals and activities in this series in particular, and with a population with special medical needs in general.

Goals

- To gain knowledge of family-school collaboration for special needs populations.
- To review a multi-family session for students with special needs.
- To apply family-school collaboration to a special needs population in participants' own schools.

Handouts/Materials

- *Activity Planning Form: Asthma Workshops*

- *Activity Planning Form (Blank)*
- White board/Smart Board or chart paper

Introduction

Say: In this session we will examine one way to apply family-school collaboration to a special needs population: elementary school children with asthma. Our overarching goal was to help children and their families find more effective ways to cope with asthma in order to improve their school attendance and performance. Ultimately, we wanted the workshops to: help families with asthmatic children make a better connection to the school, gain an understanding of how to manage the illness with cooperation from the school, and maximize students' educational and developmental potential. We hoped these families would come to view the school as an environment where problems affecting a child's attendance, achievement and social-emotional growth are solved -- not exacerbated.

Activity I. Asthma Workshop Example

INSTRUCTIONS

1. **Say: We will 'walk through' the planning and implementation phases of these meetings after a brief description of the population being served.**

   The school is a New York City elementary school in an impoverished neighborhood. The school's population is predominantly Latino with a mix of Puerto Rican families who have been in New York for several generations and more recent immigrants from the Dominican Republic and Latin America. The district in which the school is situated has the highest asthma rate among pupils in all of New York City. In an effort to connect with the families of at-risk students with poor attendance, interviews were conducted with numerous parents to determine their view of the school and the reasons for their children's absenteeism. Many of them pointed to their children's asthma as a major cause of poor attendance. They noted that they were uncertain whether it was safe to send their children to school if they had a cold or were wheezing at all. Few of the children had ongoing, consistent medical care or preventive medication for asthma.

   As a result of the interviews, two things became clear to school personnel:

- **They needed to work more collaboratively with parents of asthmatic children.**

- **It would be beneficial to offer a series of multi-family workshops about asthma and how to deal with it.**

2. Distribute *Activity Planning Form: Asthma Workshops* Handout #1.

3. Say: **Here is the activity planning form they developed. Let's read through it together. As we read it please keep the following questions in mind:**

- **What would you consider appropriate follow-up for such a series of meetings?**

- **Are there special needs populations in your school with issues for which multi-family, multi-disciplinary meetings would be helpful?**

4. Invite the group to comment on the plan including its strengths and weaknesses.

5. Ask the group to share additional ideas about follow-up to this series to insure that asthmatic children attend school more regularly.

6. *Think about it.* Ask the group to make concrete suggestions about how these ideas could be implemented and maintained, reflecting particularly on the following:

- *What is the suggested plan?*

- *What would it take to put it in place?*

- *Who would be responsible?*

- *Who would have to OK it and set it in motion?*

- *How would the plan be monitored?*

- *How often would/could the key individuals involved in the plan communicate with each other?*

Activity II. Activity Planning

INSTRUCTIONS

1. Say: **Let's return now to the questions I asked you to think about earlier:**

- **Are there issues confronting special needs populations in your school for which collaborative multi-family, multi-disciplinary meetings would be helpful?**

- **What kinds of issues came to mind as you reviewed this activity plan?**

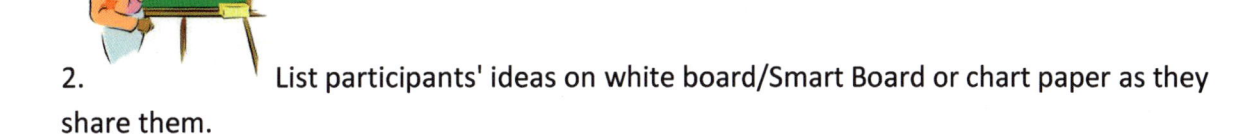

2. List participants' ideas on white board/Smart Board or chart paper as they share them.

3. Say: **Let's look over these ideas. Could we group them according to theme or topic?**

Try to group the ideas into a few broad categories. Invite participants to get into groups related to each category and brainstorm ideas for multi-family session on these topics.

4. Distribute blank *Activity Planning Form* Handout #2 to be used as a guide for discussion.

5. *Think about it.* After the groups have talked for 10 minutes ask them to consider, with the large group, the following questions as part of the planning process:

- *Who would individuals in each group need to talk to if you wanted to convene such a meeting?*

- *How would you delegate responsibility for these next steps?*

SESSION 24
Handout 1

Activity Planning Form: Asthma Workshops

INSTRUCTIONS: Use the following elements of school climate as a checklist to plan an activity to fulfill a significant educational goal or deal with a major issue of concern at your school.

Issue or Concern:
- High absenteeism among asthmatic children in the school.
- Parents' concerns about whether to send their asthmatic children to school on days they manifested some symptoms or not.
- Parents' questions about whether the school is a safe environment for asthmatic children -both as a physical setting with many staircases and possible asbestos problems, and in terms of the physical demands of gym class and recess.
- The over-protectiveness of parents of asthmatic children and their reluctance in or ignorance about helping the children act as self-managers of their asthma.

Activity:
Multi-family workshop series: "Living and Learning with Asthma: Home and School Working Together"

ELEMENTS OF CLIMATE:

Messages to be conveyed (values, norms, beliefs):
- We want to work together with you and your child to help you find ways to manage asthma so it interferes less with your child's learning and enjoyment of school.
- Your child can learn to act as a self-manager of his/her asthma.
- You and your child's teacher can work together to help reduce school-related asthma problems.
- Parents of asthmatic children can become so concerned that they help their child too much and make their child feel that his/her condition is more serious and/or dangerous than it actually is.
- You and your child can learn to discuss asthma and handle it successfully by communicating with each other.

Individuals or groups who should be involved:
- Medical personnel who specialize in childhood asthma e.g., an M.D. pediatric asthma specialist and an R.N. public health nurse with expertise in pulmonary illness.
- Students who have been identified as asthmatic
- Parents/family members of these children
- School administrative and teaching personnel
- Facilitators with expertise in family-school collaboration

Collaborative interactions necessary to reach goal and convey message:
- Opportunities for students to express their feelings about asthma and asthma attacks through drawings and discussions and to share these with their peers, families, and teachers.
- Opportunities for parents to react to their children's drawings and feelings and to hear the responses of other parents.
- Didactic presentations by medical personnel for students and parents about the physiology, causes, symptomatology and triggers of asthma.
- Discussions among children, school staff and families about the impact of asthma on students' school lives.
- Simulated experiences, such as role-plays, which allow parents and children to understand each other's experiences with asthma and which help them communicate about coping with and recognizing early warning signs of asthma attacks.
- Opportunities for children to learn how to self-manage their asthma and to know when to ask parents for help, and for parents to appreciate their children's ability to do this.
- Didactic presentations by medical personnel for student and parents about how to jointly decide when to go to school and/or to the doctor; a discussion about the purpose and use of different asthma medications.

Physical characteristics and materials that convey the message:
- Meeting held in school setting where chairs can be arranged in a circle for the adults and there is room for children to sit on the floor.
- All participants including school staff and medical personnel sit in a circle together.
- Refreshments served.
- Adults interspersed among children so that those students whose parents are not present have an adult to relate to.

SESSION 24
Handout 2

Activity Planning Form

INSTRUCTIONS: Use the following elements of school climate as a checklist to plan an activity to fulfill a significant educational goal or deal with a major issue of concern at your school.

Issue or Concern:

_____

Activity:

_____

ELEMENTS OF CLIMATE:

Messages to be conveyed (values, norms, beliefs):

_____

_____

_____

Individual and/or groups who should be involved:

_____

_____

_____

Collaborative interactions necessary to reach goal and convey message:

_____

_____

_____

Physical characteristics and materials that convey the message:

_____

_____

End of Session 24

SESSION 25: How do we embed family-school collaboration into our school's calendar?

Rationale:

The ultimate aim of CKCC is to build a shared community of family and school personnel that collaboratively support learning and social-emotional growth at home and at school. When climate building is defined narrowly as simply a series of activities, we can potentially lose sight of CKCC's critical overall objective of promoting greater inclusion and participation of parents and other family members directly in the educational process. We must maintain the perspective that collaborative climate building extends to ongoing school activities, the school curriculum, and, in essence, the way that the school as a whole does business.

Building and maintaining a collaborative climate for intra-staff relations and for family-school relations is accomplished by finding ways of embedding collaborative activities into all aspects of school life and by making such activities routine (i.e. easily repeatable year after year) and tied to learning objectives. Such routines are established over time (at least 2-3 years) as the entire school community employs family-school collaboration processes for accomplishing its goals.

Goals

- To review examples of traditional and collaborative school calendar events.
- To brainstorm ways to transform traditional events into collaborative family-school activities.

Handouts/Materials

- *Sample School Calendar – Traditional*
- *Sample School Calendar – Collaborative*
- *Creating Collaborative Events (blank)*

Introduction

Say: **Today we are going to find ways to extend family-school collaboration into all aspects of school life throughout the school year. We are going to highlight curricular themes, school activities, and the general positive tone of the school through different family-school collaborative activities. We'll explore ideas for each month or throughout the school calendar.**

Activity I. School Calendar Comparisons

INSTRUCTIONS

1. Distribute copies of *Sample School Calendar – Traditional* Handout #1.

2. Say: **Although many of these activities can be school-wide, they are not required to be so. Individual teachers or groups of teachers can develop these ideas on their own. Gradually as a critical mass of teachers implements a specific climate-building activity, that activity may be accepted as a school norm, a routine that is repeated and elaborated on each year.**

   The examples of activities listed on the next handout are just suggestions to demonstrate that collaborative activities including families, students, and staff can enhance what happens in the classroom instead of compete with it.

   The examples also demonstrate that collaboration does not necessarily mean that parents have to be "in" the school physically for a collaborative approach to problem solving to be successful. Their contribution to an ongoing interactive learning activity may be made at home and incorporated into a subsequent in-class event by the child and teacher.

   Most importantly, the activities indicate that a more interactive approach to building classroom and school activities can send a clear message to the entire family-school community that collaborative relations support children in becoming successful learners.

3. Distribute *Sample School Calendar – Collaborative* Handout #2. Ask participants to look over the examples.

4. *Think about it.* Invite participants to share reactions, reflecting on the following:

   - *How would something like this work in your schools?*

   - *What reservations do you have about this approach?*

   - *What are its strong points?*

Activity II. Generating New Ideas

INSTRUCTIONS

1. Distribute *Creating Collaborative Events* Handout #3.

2. Say: **I'd like to give you the opportunity now to develop some of your own ideas about collaborative events throughout the school calendar. Please choose one or two typical school calendar events and briefly redesign them to emphasize collaborative interaction involving children, parents and other family members, and school staff. You may want to alter these events to emphasize the collaborative family-school framework. Be sure that you envision the students as active participants in the planning, preparations and implementation of the events.**

    Before you begin let's quickly review the key components of collaborative climate building:

- It includes both parents and child as active participants.
- It sends a message of welcome, inclusion and respect.
- It demonstrates that, when families and schools jointly support a child's learning and growth, the child has higher achievement and gives more effort to his or her learning tasks.
- It utilizes the family as a resource in the learning process.
- It highlights the common concern of families and schools for the education and well being of children.

SESSION 25
Handout 1

Sample School Calendar – Traditional

SEPTEMBER: Orientation for Kindergarten/Orientation for New Parents/Meet the Teacher

OCTOBER: School Safety Month

NOVEMBER: School Wide Can Drive/School Wide Recycling Drive

DECEMBER: Multicultural Celebration

JANUARY: School Wide Reading Month/Family Reading/Family Math

FEBRUARY: Special Focus: Test Taking/Prevention of Holdovers

MARCH: Test Month

APRIL: Art/Music/Dance/Performance Fair

MAY: Family Month/Family Activities

JUNE: Transitions to New Grades/New Schools

SESSION 25
Handout 2

Sample School Calendar – Collaborative

I. *Overview*

SEPTEMBER: Orientation for Kindergarten/Orientation for New Parents/Meet the Teacher

OCTOBER: School Safety Month

NOVEMBER: School Wide Can Drive/ School Wide Recycling Drive

DECEMBER: Multicultural Celebration

JANUARY: School Wide Reading Month/Family Reading/Family Math

FEBRUARY: Special Focus: Test Taking/ Prevention of Holdovers

MARCH: Test Month

APRIL: Art/Music /Dance/Performance Fair

MAY: Family Month/Family Activities

JUNE: Transitions to New Grades/New Schools

II. *Family-School Links to Curriculum*

SEPTEMBER: Orientation
Orientation can include the children and their families in substantive roles:
- Students can demonstrate new classroom materials, e.g., the computer lab, or with younger children, show how they use their morning meeting to extend vocabulary.
- Small family groups can have discussions during the orientation meeting with suggestions of ways that parents can help children at home: contracts for homework, rules for TV, establishing goals for the new school year.

OCTOBER: School Safety Month
This can be broadened from safety tips during Halloween to include curriculum-based activities that can promote increased collaboration between home and school:
- Letters can be exchanged between home and school about school safety.
- Children can write about how they are working together to maintain safe recess periods.

- Parents and children can develop a newsletter with word games to be played in school regarding safety.
- Students can interview parents and other adults in the community and use the information to develop murals regarding safe ways to "trick or treat."
- Community leaders or police officers can visit the school to make presentations on safety issues, which generate follow-up discussions and writing between home and school.

NOVEMBER: School-Wide Can Drive

This can be expanded from a stand-alone activity to a collaborative effort integrating math, social studies and language arts:

- Students can record with their parents the numbers and types of cans they collect from home and examples of recipes in which their contents could be used.
- In class the students can graph the kinds of food collected and generate questions for their parents about why they choose to have certain types of food on hand.
- Classroom discussion can explore the themes of homelessness, the needs of the elderly and the poor. Students might discuss these topics with a few people in their families, and then compare their conversations in class.
- The class can take a trip to a soup kitchen where the cans might be donated, visit local senior citizen centers, and homeless shelters. The trips can be followed-up by letters to the centers and/or stories written about people the children meet during the trips.
- Parents can be involved via newsletters, videotaping of the visits, the creation of a special bulletin board outlining the sequence of events through pictures which families and visitors can see when they visit the school: collecting the cans at home, bringing the cans to school, counting and classifying the cans in the classroom and delivering the cans to the soup kitchens, etc.

DECEMBER: Multicultural Celebrations

Celebrations offer a wonderful opportunity to involve families beyond their traditional role as "audience" at a Holiday Assembly featuring songs from many different lands:

- Parents might organize a multicultural dinner preceded by class visits to prepare the meals in the classroom. Students could interview family members to obtain favorite holiday recipes. Then they could use math skills to adapt the recipes to make sufficient quantities for the whole class, and actually prepare a few with family members in the classroom.
- In classes with children of immigrant parents, children could gain an understanding of geography, ecology and culture by identifying the types of ingredients used in their family holiday dishes and linking these to climate and agricultural patterns of their parents' home countries.

- Students could devise interviews to administer to parents and family members about how different holidays were celebrated in their own families. Parents might share stories on videotape.
- Students and parents could jointly create their own picture books about the holidays. Parents and children might make murals including special recipes and pictures drawn by the children of making a special holiday meal.

JANUARY: School-Wide Reading Month

Reading can become a school-wide focus that promotes family-school collaboration as well as ties to class work by establishing a family reading program:

- Parents can be invited to "reading breakfasts," morning visits to read with small groups of children for the first fifteen minutes of each day.
- Parents and children can help keep lists of all the ways and times that reading goes on in their families: reading the paper, family notes, reading recipes, reading shopping circulars, letters, school newsletters, etc. These lists can become classroom graphs or murals about the importance of family reading.
- A special family reading group can be formed to develop games that parents can use with their children to promote family reading.
- Book lists can be made of all books read during the month.
- Parents can be invited into the classroom to engage in family reading activities – book making, playing games following written directions, creating raps and poems, etc. – with their children.

FEBRUARY: Focus on Test-Taking

A school might choose to improve reading scores by exhorting individual teachers to work harder, and they in turn try to inculcate the necessary skills in their students to help them pass city-, district- or state-wide tests. Family resources are rarely called into play to expand resources available to the school in preparation for these examinations. A collaborative approach might include:

- Schools can hold school-wide discussions about the relative importance of tests, the connections between tests and classroom activities and preparation for test taking.
- Panels of older students can talk to younger ones about their own experiences taking tests. Stories, audio and videotapes could be developed regarding different approaches to test taking.
- These activities in turn might inspire parents to develop tapes about their own attitudes to test taking, driving tests, civil servant tests, typing tests, professional exams, etc.
- After the tests are administered, further curriculum opportunities might be developed for students who did poorly or whose tests scores do not reflect their learning potential

e.g., changing "holdover meetings" to those meetings with learning specialists who work with the whole family.

MARCH: Test Month
The anticipation of standardized tests provides an opportunity for children and their families to work together with the teacher to find ways to decrease stress, improve study habits, and discuss each other's concerns about anxiety-producing topics:
- A school might involve families and students in test-prep workshops called "Getting Ready for Standardized Tests."
- Prior to meeting with their children, parents could meet with the guidance counselor to discuss their anxieties and raise questions about testing. The guidance counselor can help allay parental fears and might even teach parents stress reduction techniques such as relaxation, deep breathing, and imagery work that they can utilize for themselves and with their children.
- Parents and children might share their concerns about testing with each other and report out to the whole group. As the teacher lists these concerns, the group identifies and addresses themes that emerge.
- The teacher, families, and students can discuss how they might handle stress, identify the most effective ways to coordinate preparation at home and school, and develop rituals which help them ease anxiety. Adults could practice with their children the stress reduction skills they've just learned.
- Teachers can prepare vignettes of hypothetical situations around which students and families can develop skits about the "dos" and "don'ts" of test preparation.

APRIL: Art and Music Fair
These fairs often reinforce the view of families as "audience." To develop a more collaborative approach to such events:
- Children can interview all the members of their families to find out who plays an instrument, sings, or likes to draw.
- Classes can choose different classroom activities such as writing one's own songs or studying the mathematical aspects of certain types or pieces of music, and invite parents to participate in creative assignments related to these endeavors.
- When possible, parents can contribute their own music skills or artwork to the fair towards a goal such as raising funds for the school music program.

MAY: Family Month
Creating a "Family Month" in lieu of Mother's Day or Father's Day opens up a wide variety of classroom activities. It also affirms the reality that families come in many shapes, sizes and colors:
- Classes can study jobs in a family, ways of sharing feelings like humor or anger within the family, favorite foods, songs or stories in the family. This new information in turn can be used to develop new murals, stories, books and tapes.
- Students can discuss questions they have about their backgrounds and develop interviews to administer to key family members. They can create stories, plays and/or murals based on the information they collect.
- Special family traditions such as coming of age rituals might be the focus of an older group, while a younger group might explore the challenges of various changes in families.

JUNE: Transitions to New Grades/New Schools
Transitions to new grades or a new school too often occur haphazardly. Family-school collaboration can lead to smoother, more exciting, and better-informed transitions for parents and children alike:
- Older children in a school can host a visiting day for younger children and their families who may be attending that school next year. Panel discussions by older students can help students know what to expect, and parents and teachers together can help children formulate questions for the panelists in order to help younger students articulate their concerns.
- If the transition involves choosing a school, a School Choice Fair can be organized in a convenient community setting. Children can prepare books citing the characteristics and advantages of their school.
- With new information, children can write about their feelings about attending a new class or new school.
- Parents can work together to develop transportation teams for the new school before the first day.
- Transition difficulties can be normalized through anticipatory discussions that allow children and parents to talk together about what they anticipate may happen in the new setting and what they fear and/or look forward to.
- Transition buddies (students and parents from the new school) can help ameliorate some of the stresses of moving to a new school for both the graduating child and his/her family.
- Graphs can be developed and expanded as part of the on-going problem-solving approach, listing strategies for successful transitions to a new school (i.e., graph cites how many plan to use that particular strategy).

SESSION 25
Handout 3

Creating Collaborative Events

Original School Calendar Event	Collaborative School Calendar Event

End of Session 25

Section 6
Sustaining the Momentum: Deepening Investment

I. Making It Stick: Institutionalizing Collaboration

SESSION 26: How can we institutionalize a collaborative approach?

Rationale:

There are three prerequisites for successful institutionalization of a collaborative approach to planning and problem solving. When these three preconditions are fulfilled, schools are able to restructure their existing activities and initiate other activities that will promote family-school partnerships to support the education of all students.

Goals

- To identify prerequisites for successful institutionalization of family-school collaboration.
- To create an action plan for institutionalizing family-school collaboration.
- To recognize opportunities to informally promote family-school collaboration.

Handouts/Materials

- *Three Preconditions for Institutionalizing Family-School Collaboration*
- *Worksheet for Institutionalizing Family-School Collaboration*
- *Activity Planning Form*
- White board/Smart Board or chart paper

Introduction

Say: In previous sessions, we have explored various approaches to family-school collaboration. If this approach is going to actually take hold and be utilized systematically in your district at large, there are some key elements that must be in place. Today we are going to discuss ways to institutionalize family-school collaboration in your district, as a way of doing business across many schools.

Activity I. Preconditions for Institutionalizing Family-School Collaboration

INSTRUCTIONS

1. Say: **Today we will consider institutionalization of family-school collaboration on two levels. The first is the formal or structural level where new roles and decision-making bodies are formed. The second is the informal level where new opportunities for family-school collaboration are identified in the course of routine discussions about curriculum, discipline, community relations, grading, transitions, school-wide events, etc. Increasingly, on both levels, people get the idea that collaboration is a way of conducting business. We'll talk about both of these levels today.**

   Let's first consider the need to institutionalize family-school collaboration. What happens if a culture of collaboration is not integrally woven into the structure of the school system?

2. *Think about it.* Ask participants to think of innovative programs in which they have previously participated and reflect on the following:

   - *What happened to the programs after the consultants/change agents left the district?*

   - *What would have changed the outcome?*

3. Distribute *Preconditions for Institutionalizing Family-School Collaboration* Handout #1. Ask participants to read the handout and indicate why these three preconditions are especially important. What is the value of each of the three to family-school collaboration?

291

4. *Think about it.* Ask participants to reflect on the following:

- *What is the value of each of the three preconditions to family-school collaboration?*

- *Can you imagine the first two in place at the building level without the third at the district level?*

- *Could family-school collaboration be institutionalized in that case? How?*

5. Invite a show of hands among participants in terms of whether they think each of the three preconditions already exists fully, somewhat, or not at all in their district/school. On chart paper indicate in columns labeled "Already Exists," "Exists Somewhat," and "Doesn't Exist At All" for each precondition. Then tally the results for each precondition and discuss with the group why some seem more difficult to implement than others. Brainstorm general ways of dealing with some of the obstacles that are identified.

Activity II. Ways of Introducing Family-School Collaboration

INSTRUCTIONS

1. Ask participants to divide into small groups by school. If they are all from the same school or the same few schools, then they can just divide into several small groups.

2. Say: **You are going to have the opportunity to create an Action Plan for institutionalizing family-school collaboration in your school and/or district. Please be sure to list the suggestions and actions you decide on so you leave today's session with concrete ideas about what each of you can do.**

3. Distribute *Worksheet for Institutionalizing Family-School Collaboration* Handout #2. Instruct participants to assess – based on the previous discussion – where their school is currently vis-a-vis the three preconditions, and what it would take to move forward on each of the three.

4. *Think about it.* Have participants report the following out to the large group, giving them an opportunity to identify strategies presented by other groups that might work in their situation as well:

- *How can the people in your group begin the process of institutionalizing family-school collaboration at the school (and/or district) level?*

- *What specific actions can each of you take to establish each of the three conditions we've discussed?*

Have small groups report out to the large group and give participants an opportunity to identify strategies presented by other groups that might work in their situation as well.

Activity III. Listening with a "Collaborative Ear"

INSTRUCTIONS

1. **Say: As we mentioned earlier, the second means of institutionalizing family-school collaboration is introduced informally by modeling how to incorporate collaboration routinely into the planning of new programs, special events, and problem-solving tasks. As professionals with an understanding and appreciation for collaborative processes, you can help others in your school and/or district begin to think in more collaborative ways. One way of doing this is to hear with a collaborative "ear" when you attend different types of meetings -- to participate in discussions with an ear towards unrecognized opportunities for family-school collaboration.**

   As you participate in various committees and meetings, ask yourself:
   - **"How might family-school collaboration be a means to accomplishing this goal?"**
   - **"What special benefits would be achieved by using family-school partnership in this arena?"**

   We are going to practice this skill now. Think of this activity as "agility training." Your task is to quickly formulate suggestions you might offer to help your group see opportunities for incorporating family-school collaboration into a new activity or program they are planning, or a particular problem they are trying to solve.

   I am going to describe a few hypothetical committee meetings. After I do so, please quickly jot down some suggestions you might make.

2. Read the following examples to the group one at a time. Give them a minute or two to reflect and write down their suggestions before moving on to the next example.

   - **Example 1:** Staff Committee developing a plan for mainstreaming special education students.
   - **Example 2:** Staff Committee developing a school-wide discipline policy to deal with unruly behavior.
   - **Example 3:** Staff Committee developing content themes for a magnet school program.
   - **Example 4:** Staff Committee developing a "Library Power" program to encourage reading successes.
   - **Example 5:** Staff Committee considering the introduction of a new hands-on elementary school science curriculum.

3. Reporting Out:

Invite participants to share their suggestions for each example with the group. Summarize the importance of their ideas by noting what has been added to the conception of each task by making family-school collaboration a significant aspect of each program. *Make clear that the purpose is not to find "something for parents to do." Rather we want to use the active engagement of staff, students, and family members to foster learning and to maximize resources to support children's learning and growth.* Encourage them to practice listening with a collaborative ear the next time they are in a committee or staff meeting.

Activity IV. Practice for Key Conversations

INSTRUCTIONS

1. Distribute *Activity Planning Form* Handout #3. Read over the form and specifically the section entitled People and Groups. Think about the people with whom you will need to connect regarding this activity.

2. *Think about it.* Ask participants to reflect on the following:

- *Who is the first person that you need to talk with about implementing this activity?*

- *What are you asking this person to do?*

- *What is your goal?*

3. Break into dyads and label each partnership as A and B. First, Person A directs B who to be in a role-play. Person A practices this first conversation using the activity that is being planned.

4. Ask participants who were B in this activity to report to the group what they found to be most persuasive about approaching this task with an emphasis on family-school collaboration. Also, what did your partner say that made you skeptical and what would increase your willingness to go ahead?

5. Have the dyads reverse roles and incorporate this new feedback into their approach.

SESSION 26
Handout 1

Three Preconditions for Institutionalizing Family-School Collaboration

1. The district **superintendent** (at the district level) and/or school **principal** (at the individual school level) must show a high level of commitment to family-school collaboration. This high level of commitment must be conveyed to school staff, parents, and children, and their interest and input should be requested.

2. At the **school-wide level**, a **Collaboration Committee** optimally comprised of the principal, school support staff (psychologist, social worker, and guidance counselor), teachers, and parents should be put in place. This committee takes primary responsibility for planning and coordinating the implementation of activities aimed at building family-school partnerships. The committee is chaired by a **Family-School Facilitator** who initiates, organizes and facilitates activities that enhance family-school relationships. The committee, under the leadership of the Facilitator, commences the needs assessment process and makes decisions about the pacing of the collaborative change process. The committee also makes decisions about who to train and how and when training should take place. Lastly, committee members are critical decision-makers regarding the evaluation and feedback process. In essence, this committee represents the core collaborative team that works together and with others and mirrors collaboration to the rest of the school staff, parents, and children.

3. At the **district or network-wide level**, a **Family-School Coordinator** is a necessary position for the coordination of family-school collaborative activities and meetings across schools.

SESSION 26
Handout 2

Worksheet for Institutionalizing Family-School Collaboration

Readiness of our school/district to institutionalize necessary structure or roles

I. Indicate below whether the precondition exists at all and, if so, how established it is.

    1. High level of principal/superintendent commitment to collaborative family-school partnerships

    _____

    _____

    2. Collaboration committee

    _____

    _____

    3. District-level family-school coordinator/school-based family-school facilitator

    _____

    _____

II. Where appropriate, indicate below what needs to happen to implement each precondition and what might get in the way.

    1. _____

    _____

    2. _____

    _____

    3. _____

    _____

On the back of the page list your names and indicate what each of you intends to do to institutionalize each of the preconditions. Determine a time when you can touch base to discuss your progress and continue planning.

SESSION 26
Handout 3

Activity Planning Form: Institutionalizing a Collaborative Approach

INSTRUCTIONS: Use the following elements of school climate as a checklist to plan an activity to fulfill a significant educational goal or deal with a major issue of concern at your school.

Issue or Concern: _____

Activity: _____

ELEMENTS OF CLIMATE:

Messages to be conveyed (values, norms, beliefs):

_____
_____
_____
_____

Individual and/or groups who should be involved:

_____
_____
_____
_____

Collaborative interactions necessary to reach goal and convey message:

_____
_____
_____

Physical characteristics of the environment and materials that convey message:

_____
_____
_____

End of Session 26

II. Action Research: Reflective Conversations about Collaboration

SESSION 27: What is an "action research approach" to feedback of evaluation research?

Rationale:

Often in educational restructuring, evaluation becomes the final stage in the change process. Experts evaluate the change efforts, and outcomes are presented as *a fait accompli*. Participants rarely have the opportunity to interact with and/or consider the implications of the evaluation results for their professional lives. Often they see an evaluation as a way of identifying their deficiencies and their failures to obtain program goals.

This session tries to alter the fundamental assumptions about the purpose and use of educational assessment and evaluation research. Rather than see it as an end in itself, we see it as a part of the ongoing collaborative change process – as a basis for participants' exploration of where they are and as a jumping off point for decisions about where they want to be. Evaluation becomes the springboard for action.

The key goal is for the staff to own the data – to play an active role in its analysis and application. Rather than tell them what it means, we ask them to react to and interpret it in light of their experience in the school. In other words, they become partners and experts in the evaluation process. To do so however, requires that data collection and feedback be neither threatening nor blaming. Rather, the process must show respect for the staff's opinions and incorporate negative as well as positive reactions.

This session of the manual will illustrate the use of data as an intervention. It will demonstrate how to present data in its least threatening form and how to help staff members who may be unfamiliar with research results come to see analysis as an opportunity for self-assessment and for participation in reflective conversations that deepen their school's commitment to family-school collaboration.

Goals

- To learn to use research findings to further build a collaborative climate.
- To explore non-threatening ways of presenting evaluation results to school staff.
- To understand how to interpret, draw implications, and build actions from evaluation findings.

Handouts/Materials

- *Stages of the Research Process*
- *Sample Data Page for Interpretation*
- *Sample Data Summary Page*
- White board/Smart Board or chart paper

Introduction

Say: **Today we are going to explore new ways in which you as educators can use research findings to help you (and families and students) build a collaborative climate in your school.**

I'm sure many of you have had the typical teacher/school person's experience with evaluators or researchers. They come to the school, sit in your classroom and observe or interview you and your students, thank you and leave. Sometimes they provide a written or oral report of their findings and answer your questions about their results. But rarely do they offer you the opportunity to explore or respond to the data yourself or to discuss its implications with colleagues, families or students – to make the results meaningful to you in your work.

In this session, we'll walk through a different kind of data analysis experience and discuss ways for you to work more collaboratively with evaluators/researchers.

Activity I. Reflection on Past Experiences

INSTRUCTIONS

1. Say: **How many of you have had experiences with researchers/evaluators similar to the one I described? Have any of you had different experiences?**

2. Have individuals share different experiences with the group.

3. Say: **What were the most and least helpful aspects of your experiences?**

4. List responses on chart paper and identify themes that emerge. Some examples of themes under most helpful aspects might be:

> - I learned something new about my students or myself as a teacher.
> - I discovered areas where things were going better (worse) than I thought.
> - I could see the classroom/school from a different perspective.
> - I realized that the changes I am trying to make are slowly beginning to make a difference.

5. Some examples of themes under least helpful aspects might be:

> - They answered their *own* questions, not ones that were relevant to me in my work.
> - They told us what they had found but didn't give us an opportunity to think about it.
> - I am not sure what the implications of their findings are for my day-to-day work.
> - There was no chance to discuss differences or disagreements with their results.

6. Summarize the themes with the participants and indicate issues that seem to emerge most prominently. Two of them might be:

> - Lack of meaningful participation in shaping questions or responding to findings.
> - Feeling judged rather than informed or collaborated with.

Activity II. Stages of the Research Process

INSTRUCTIONS

1. Say: **There are different ways of doing research/evaluation and different kinds of partnerships that can be established. Many of you may have heard about or had exposure to the "teacher as researcher approach" which is gaining momentum nationally. Yet even without teachers actually acting as researchers, they can have a meaningful role in the research process at every stage. Let's think about the stages of the research process and discuss ways in which teachers/school staff could collaborate with researchers/evaluators at each one.**

2. Distribute *Stages of the Research Process* Handout #1. Ask participants to get into 6 small groups. Explain that each group is going to consider how they as school personnel could/would want to be involved in one stage of the research process. Assign one stage to each group.

After 5-10 minutes invite the small groups to report out.

3. Say: **Let's go over each stage. For the first stage, "identifying the problem," what role could you as school staff play during this stage to make it more collaborative and meaningful to you?**
Responses might include:

- Being consulted about what issues to investigate in the first place.

For the second stage, "developing and clarifying the research question," what roles did your group discuss?
Responses might include:

- Being asked by researchers/evaluators what they would like to know about specific issues being investigated.
- Being invited to suggest which questions would be most directly meaningful and applicable to their work.

For the third stage, "designing data collection strategies and instruments," how could you be involved in this stage of the process?

Responses might include:

- Acting as sounding boards about effectiveness of proposed interview and survey questions based on intimate knowledge of the school, its students and parents.
- Helping to develop questions that might inform classroom practice.
- Having a say in which questions or types of questions would be culturally meaningful and developmentally appropriate.

Let's look at the fourth stage: "collection of data." How, if at all, would you like to be involved in this stage of the research process?

Responses might include:

- Helping to collect the data by interviewing students, colleagues or parents.
- Identifying representative samples of students to be interviewed, e.g., recent arrivals in the U.S. vs. students who have been here for several years.
- Assisting in the preparation of students for data collection, e.g., insuring that permission slips are signed, discussing the process with students to alleviate anxiety.
- Cooperating in the interview/survey process.

Next, let's move on to stage five: "answering the question: analyzing and interpreting the data." What ideas did you have for how you might be involved here?

Responses might include:

- Viewing the raw data, or a simple summary of the data, before it is analyzed.
- Being invited to help analyze the data.
- Having the opportunity to consider the meaning and interpretation of the data rather than having it presented to us by others.

Finally, let's think about the last stage: "considering implications and raising new questions."

Responses might include:

- Being invited to have a discussion with the researchers/evaluators and each other about the findings.
- Having the opportunity to respond to the findings and their implications in light of our own experiences.
- Being able to use the data for something meaningful to our work, e.g., new approaches to family events, future planning, different program strategies etc.

After all the groups have reported out, ask the participants how many actually would like to be involved in more collaborative efforts with researchers, and if they would, what channels exist in their schools for making this happen?

Activity III. Data Feedback Process

INSTRUCTIONS

1. Explain to the group that we are now going to experience one aspect of collaborative work with research/evaluation efforts.

2. Say: **We are going to walk through a data feedback process that has been utilized in many schools working to achieve family-school collaboration.**

The data we will be working with today is from a New York City elementary school which implemented a new elective activity: Multi-Family Problem-Solving Meetings for students in danger of being held over or of being dropped from the intellectually gifted (Eagle) program.

The meetings were successful in decreasing the number of holdovers and demotions from the Eagle program. However, the teachers wondered if the students were frightened or intimidated by the sessions and requested that the family-school consultants assess their pupils' reactions to the meetings. An interview addressing the issues of most concern to the staff was designed and administered to the students. After the data was initially analyzed, it was presented to the school staff in its most accessible, least complicated form – a summary of the data for each question was presented directly on the interview protocol under that question. The language used was non-technical and understandable to school staff.

We will simulate the process the teachers at this school experienced with a few of the questions so you have a clear idea of how this type of feedback session works.

The goal of this meeting is for the staff to have the opportunity to:
- **Summarize the findings**
- **Interact with and react to the data themselves**
- **Consider implications of the findings for their next steps with this issue**

3. Distribute *Sample Data Page for Interpretation* Handout #2. Explain that in an actual session, staff would be divided into pairs and each pair would be responsible for analyzing, drawing implications about, and summarizing one or two questions for their colleagues.

4. Explain that in this instance we'll all focus on the same sample question- question #4. Ask each person first to read and reflect on the questions individually. They are to:

- **Put a "+" next items which stand out in a positive way**
- **Put a "-" next to items which concern them or which they think need to be improved**
- **Put a "*" next to items which surprise or confuse them**

5. Next, they are to discuss their reactions with a partner.

6. Explain that if they were doing a complete survey, they would prepare an informal summary of the most significant findings and their reactions to share with the group. The group would then discuss implications of the findings, brainstorm next steps and identify specific individuals to be in charge of implementing these.

7. Ask a few of the pairs to share their summaries and reactions. List their remarks on large chart paper by question, creating spaces for summaries and positive and negative reactions.

8. *Think about it.* Ask the group to consider what stood out in their responses to these few questions:

- *If they were teachers or staff in this school, what activities or organizational procedures could they devise to address these issues?*

- *What would they consider the most important next steps?*

9. Say: **Here's what the staff at that school discovered from their analysis of the data for Question #4.**

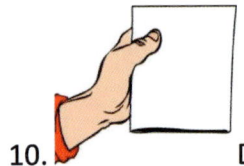

10. Distribute *Sample Question for Data Analysis* Handout #3.

11. Say: **As a follow-up to this meeting, the Facilitator compiled the information gathered into typed lists indicating which reactions and issues were most commonly cited by staff. That list and the ideas for next steps with specific dates for follow-up meetings were then circulated among the staff as a way of keeping the issues alive and preparing for subsequent meetings. As a result of these meetings, the staff developed routines for informing students about the meetings and helping families prepare children well ahead of time, thereby allaying their anxieties about attending such a session.**

12. *Think about it.* Once the exercise is completed ask the group to consider the following questions:

- *How beneficial do you think this experience would be for the staff in your school?*

- *How would/could it alter the staff's experience with researchers/evaluations?*

- *What would make it more worthwhile for your school?*

- *How could you work more collaboratively?*

- *Do you have researchers/evaluators working with your school? What would it take to change the way things are currently done? Who would you have to talk to first?*

SESSION 27
Handout 1

Stages of the Research Process

I. Identifying the problem

II. Developing and clarifying a research question

III. Determining and designing data collection strategies

IV. Investigating the research question: Collecting data

V. Answering the research question: Analyzing and interpreting data

VI. Considering implications and raising new questions

SESSION 27
Handout 2

Sample Question for Data Interpretation
Results from Student Interviews
Question about the Holdover/Eagle Meeting

Introduction for the Child: *One of the things that's especially interesting to me about this school is that some kids were invited to a meeting about the possibility of being held over or taken out of Eagle. I'd like to talk with you about that meeting now. Is that OK?*

4) What was your reaction when you first heard about the meeting?

   42% of the students said they were nervous or scared.

   62% were scared of the consequences of the meeting i.e., that they would be held over or taken out of Eagle as a result of the meeting.

   37% were scared about being embarrassed, publicly quizzed, or humiliated during the meeting. They feared:
   "being asked 'hard questions'"
   "being embarrassed in front of people" and
   "having my mother (say) I don't listen in front of 25 people."

   36% said they were surprised and didn't know why they had to attend the meeting or what would happen. They noted:
   "I didn't know what the hell it was going to be about."
   "Didn't know what was going to happen to me."
   "Didn't know why I had to go there."
   "Thought like I took one of those tests and didn't do good."
   "Knew my mother was going to a meeting but not me."

   21% said they wanted to go or were happy about going.

   5% said they didn't want to go.

Many of the students interviewed said they did not learn about the meeting until that day or the day before:

   36% said they first learned about the meeting on the day of the meeting.

   5% said they first learned about it the day before the meeting.

SESSION 27
Handout 3

Summary of Staff Interpretation of Holdover Meeting Data
Data Feedback Session about Students' Interviews

The following is a summary of the staff interpretations of one question on the student interview that staff analyzed at our Data Feedback Meeting.

Second, fourth and fifth grades were interviewed in June about their inclusion in the February grade level promotion and Eagle meetings.

At the feedback meeting, staff dyads summarized and discussed the findings for one question. They then reported out to the group. The following is a list of the staff's findings, reactions and comments on the data:

Question 4:

4) What was your reaction when you first heard about the meeting?

Findings:
- There was confusion about the unknown.
- A lack of communication between children, parents, teachers.
- Misinterpretation of what the meeting was to be about.

Reactions:
- No one was prepared properly. It was a new experience for everyone which led to confusion, negative apprehension, and worries of humiliation.
- Next year we could clarify in advance the purpose of the meeting in a positive way.
- We need to clarify what the format of the meeting would be in terms of what kids would be asked to do.
- Who should be responsible for communicating to children about family-school events?
- There needs to be more preparation before meetings.

End of Session 27

REFERENCES

Research Reviews

Mapp, K.L., & Henderson, A.T., (2002). A new wave of evidence: The impact of school, family, and community connections on student achievement. Austin, TX: Southwest Educational Development Laboratory.

Boethel, M., Adelman, H., Epstein, J. L., et al (2003) Diversity: School, Family, and Community Connections. Austin, TX: Southwest Educational Development Laboratory.

"Portraits of Four Schools: Meeting the Needs of Immigrant Students and their Families." The Center in Child Development and Social Policy, Yale University.
http://www.yale.edu/21C

Research-Based Reports and Articles

American Association of School Administrators. (1998). Promoting Parent Involvement. Leader's Edge, 2(2).

Dodd, A.W. & Konzal, J.L. (1999). Making our high schools better: how parents and teachers can work together. Gordonsville, VA: St. Martin's Press.

Epstein, J.L. (1995). School, family, community partnerships: caring for the children we share. Phi Delta Kappan, 76, 701-712.

Epstein, J.L., Coates, L., Salinas, K.C., Sanders, M.G. & Simon, B.S. (1997). School, Family and Community Partnerships: Your Handbook for Action. Corwin Press, Inc: Thousand Oaks, CA.

Giles, H. (1998). Parent engagement as a school reform strategy. ERIC Clearinghouse on Urban Education. Number 135.

Henderson, A. & Berla, N. (1994). A new generation of evidence: the family is critical to student achievement. National Committee for Citizens in Education.

The National Network of Partnership Schools. (2000). A model for family-school-community partnerships. Harvard Family Research Project.

Inger, Morton. (1992). Increasing the school involvement of Hispanic parents. ERIC Clearinghouse on Urban Education. Number 80.

Jordan, C., Orozco, E., Averett, J. & Buttram, J. (2001). Emerging issues in school, family and community connections. Southwest Educational Development Laboratory.

Smalley, S.Y. & Reyes-Blanes, M.E. (2001). Reaching out to African American parents in an urban community: a community-university partnership. Urban Education, 36, 518-533.

School Climate

Tagiuri, R. (1968). The concept of organizational climate. In R. Tagiuri & G. H. Litwin (Eds.), Organizational climate: Exploration of a concept (pp. 11–32). Boston: Harvard University Press.

Weiss, Howard M. and Edwards, Martha E. (1992). Family-school collaboration project: An organizational intervention model, in Sandra Christenson and Jane Close Conoley, eds., Home-School Collaboration: Building a Fundamental Educational Resource. National Association of School Psychologists.

Printed in Germany
by Amazon Distribution
GmbH, Leipzig